CW01647759

THE STORY OF
LONDON'S UNDERGROUND

An early lithograph showing Praed Street junction, Paddington, on the Metropolitan Railway. The train of 'Long Charley' coaches is hauled by a Gooch 2-4-0 tank locomotive. Outside cylinders were used to allow room for condensing tanks between the frames. The lack of protection for the enginemen was intended to avoid any risk of their view being obscured by condensation on glass in the tunnels. The artist showed the junction as designed, but when built, the mixed gauge was not extended to the Inner Circle Western Extension in the foreground

The story of London's Underground

John R. Day
MCIT Assoc IRSE

London Transport
55 Broadway
Westminster SW1

© London Transport 1963

First published 1963
This edition 1979

Photographs by
Colin Tait, H. Zinram, Topical Press, W. Curtin, Dorretts, Lenshart, and Brooks Photography.

Plate 1 is reproduced from the *Illustrated London News* of 27 December 1862

0 85329 094 6

Printed in Great Britain
by Staples Printers Ltd., London and
Rochester, Kent,
for the Publicity Office,
London Transport

AUTHOR'S NOTE

'The story of London's Underground' was written, originally, for the Underground Centenary of 1963. Since then it has passed through six editions and several reprints and, for a book sold mainly through London Transport channels, has become a minor best seller. In the course of time it has been enlarged and revised to keep in step with events since 1963 and has acquired a comprehensive index which many people have told me has greatly increased its usefulness.

This book is a concise history of London's Underground; readers who are interested in the whole scope of London's transport will find it well worthwhile to read also 'A History of London Transport' by T. C. Barker and Michael Robbins.

The inclusion of this note allows me to thank all those inside and outside London Transport who have helped with information and ideas over the years. They are too many to list individually, but I must mention two in particular – the late T. S. Lascelles, Past President of the Institution of Railway Signal Engineers, and Charles E. Lee, whose services to transport history need no panegyrics from me.

JOHN R. DAY

ENFIELD, 1978

CONTENTS

I The Coming of the Metropolitan

JUST AS main-line railways first came to full flower in Great Britain, so did underground railways. Well over a hundred years ago, on 10 January 1863, the world's first public passenger-carrying underground railway, the Metropolitan, opened the gates of its stations to Londoners. Its route from Bishop's Road, Paddington, to Farringdon Street at the City boundary was only some 3¾ miles long, but there were queues at Farringdon Street on the first day to see the new marvel. More than £850 was taken in fares that day, and two months after it opened this small steam-operated line was carrying passengers at the rate of 2¾ million a year for every mile of track; 26,500 passengers a day used it in the first six months.

Even this modest line was the end-product of a long period of planning, counter-planning, struggles, and financial manoeuvres, and the devoted propaganda of one or two men. In the 1830s, a scheme for an underground railway from King's Cross to Snow Hill (near St. Bartholomew's Hospital in the City) was put forward. Not a great deal is known about this scheme, or of another tunnel idea of the same period which might have put the London terminus of the London & Birmingham Railway on the banks of the Thames instead of at Euston; but they fired the imagination of Charles Pearson, later to become City Solicitor, and of John Hargrave Stevens, who was to be Architect and Surveyor to the City (Western Division). These two men were to press for an underground railway for London for the next 25 years or so.

In the mid 1840s there was much talk of railways to reach London, and the Great Northern Railway, an amalgamation of the Direct Northern and the London & York, was authorized by an Act of 1846. These events, together with what would now be called town-planning proposals to improve London in the area between Clerkenwell Green and Holborn Hill, brought a burst of activity from Pearson. He wrote a pamphlet which put forward the idea of a covered way down the Fleet Valley through which trains could be drawn by atmospheric power. This was at the time when experiments with this potentially powerful, clean, and silent form of motive power were being made by the London & Croydon Railway between Croydon and New Cross, and the Windsor, Staines, Brentford & London Atmospheric Railway was proposing to bring its trains to Knightsbridge and give 'ample accommodation for transit' between Buckingham Palace and Windsor Castle. It was not until the collapse of Brunel's 'Atmospheric Caper' on the South Devon Railway in 1848 shocked railway promoters and engineers – and shareholders – that atmospheric traction went out of favour.

Lack of money for the Clerkenwell town-planning scheme brought the City into the picture again in 1851, and its financial help for the scheme gave Pearson, ably assisted by Stevens, another opportunity of putting his case for the railway. Other factors in its favour at that time were that the Great Northern, already at Maiden Lane, was just building its permanent terminus at King's Cross and that the Great Western, far out in the (then) suburbs along the New Road at Paddington, was thought likely to jump at the chance of a close approach to the City.

In 1851 a committee was set up to examine Pearson's 'Railway Terminus and City Improvement Plan'. The plan consisted in essence of a 100-ft. wide road to be built from Holborn Hill, which the new Farringdon Street had reached from Fleet Street in 1830, to King's Cross. The road would be supported on the arches of a tunnel which would be wide enough for six standard-gauge and two broad-gauge railway tracks – the latter presumably aimed at enlisting the support of the Great Western, despite the gap between King's Cross and Paddington. A connection with the Great Northern was proposed at a point about a quarter of a mile north of King's Cross and at the other end of the line would be the City Terminus itself. Main-line stations were to be built on both sides of Farringdon Street, a large goods yard was to be provided, and there would be a special station for short-distance travellers. The plan, after able lobbying by Pearson and his friends, was agreed by the committee and put to the Common Council, who also approved. The main-line railways, however, were not interested, and Pearson and his associates of the City Terminus Company were left to keep their plan alive as best they could.

Meanwhile, the remoteness of Paddington had set other, more hardened, minds thinking. The Bayswater, Paddington & Holborn Bridge Railway was promoted to link Paddington with King's Cross and with Pearson's line to Farringdon. Taking advantage of the presence of the wide, reasonably straight New Road route, the cost of this line, despite its greater length, was estimated as only half that of Pearson's. Furthermore, the traffic potential of the route had been proved by the buses, and the railway could hardly fail to be a success. John Hargrave Stevens became the surveyor of this line, and one of the sponsors was William Burchell, a member of the City Terminus Company and a solicitor. Another sponsor was John Parson, whose activities with the Oxford, Worcester & Wolverhampton Railway ('Old Worse and Worse') were fresh in mind. The well-known contractors, Peto & Betts, who had worked on the O.W. & W.R. (on part of it after a pitched battle in which 2,000 navvies under the personal leadership of Brunel threw the previous contractor off the site) also put money into the railway. The engineer was John (later Sir John) Fowler, who had taken over from Brunel on the O.W. & W.R. in the spring of 1852. The first chairman of the new company was William Malins, who always declared that he had first thought of the idea of a railway under the New Road and spent a great deal of money later in trying to prove it and claim compensation from the new railway. These experts went about the job of promoting the line with smooth efficiency. Small concessions were made here and there, and plans were altered a little to meet objections. The advantages of the line were put, salesman fashion, into the ears of local authorities. The Bill went through the committee stage in Parliament in one day in 1853 without a single objection. Its Act secured, and renamed the North Metropolitan, the company began to look round for its capital.

Meanwhile, Pearson had the mortification of seeing his Bill thrown out without even a Second Reading. This did not suit the North Metropolitan, which wanted the Pearson line as an essential part of its own scheme. The experts went to work, and Pearson's scheme was subjected to corrective surgery, one of the first stages being the amputation of the 20-acre City Terminus itself, the most important part of Pearson's proposals. The route of the line was changed to allow it to serve the General Post Office and thus gain G.P.O. support.

There was opposition in Parliament, but Rowland Hill himself backed the scheme on behalf of the Post Office, and Brunel and Hawkshaw, both famous and respected engineers, supported Fowler. Malins put up a remarkable performance before the Committee, and an Act eventually emerged in 1854 for the 'Metropolitan Railway: Paddington and the Great Western Railway, the General Post Office, the London & North Western Railway, and the Great Northern

Railway'. John Fowler was named as engineer and John Hargrave Stevens as architect.

The Metropolitan now had to find the money to build its line, but the Crimean War was in progress and money was short. Eventually, however, Pearson, still eager for even his truncated scheme to be built, advised the company that if it stepped in quickly it might be able to buy, cheaply, land which had been cleared for the Clerkenwell scheme. If the company moved at once, it could get it at a reasonable price before the land was redeveloped. Although it took a threat to wind up the company to do it, and much advocacy by Pearson and others, the City Corporation eventually agreed to subscribe for shares to the value of £200,000. The Metropolitan, as we can now call it, for so it was renamed in 1854, agreed to cut the cost of the line to £950,000 by not building the section from Cowcross Street to the Post Office. It also agreed to build a line from the Great Northern so that cattle slaughtered at Copenhagen cattle market, which had taken the place of the former live cattle market at Smithfield, could be brought by the railway to Smithfield for sale. Another £175,000 was to come from the Great Western Railway in return for connecting the line to the G.W.R. and building it on the broad gauge.

This time there was enough money to make a start, and contractors were appointed. The line east of Euston Square was in the hands of John Jay, who had built the cuttings for the Great Northern Railway's route to Maiden Lane, and the line west of Euston Square, after an abortive acceptance by R. Brotherhood, was given to Smith & Knight. The Smith & Knight section ran mostly through gravel and was 'cut-and-cover'. It was crossed at Baker Street by a minor river used as a sewer, the Tybourne. Jay's section was in open cutting for a good deal of its length but included the 728 yd. Clerkenwell tunnel as well as three crossings of the Fleet River, which carried a respectable flow of water.

In 'cut-and-cover' construction, a great trench is cut for the railway and afterwards roofed over, leaving the line in a subway or covered way, the roof of which can form a road or be used for other purposes. If the roof is made strong enough, buildings can span the tracks where required. To save disturbance of property, as much of the Metropolitan Railway's trench as possible was dug along the line of existing streets – Praed Street, Marylebone Road, Euston Road, King's Cross Road, and Farringdon Road. This had some disadvantages, because beneath the surface of the roads lay nests of pipes – water, gas, and sewerage in particular as well as, even in those days, the electric telegraph. All these had to be diverted before the trench for the railway could be made.

By March 1860 the contractors were ready to start on the building. In his book *Our Iron Roads* (fifth edition, 1884), Frederick S. Williams gave a graphic description of the start of the work:

'A few wooden houses on wheels first made their appearance, and planted themselves by the gutter; then came some wagons loaded with timber and accompanied by sundry gravel-coloured men with picks and shovels. A day or two afterwards a few hundred yards of roadway were enclosed, the ordinary traffic being, of course, driven into the side streets; then followed troops of navvies, horses and engines arrived, who soon disappeared within the enclosure and down the shafts. The exact operations could be but dimly seen or heard from the street by the curious observer who gazed between the tall boards that shut him out; but paterfamilias, from his house hard by, could look down on an infinite chaos of timber, shaft holes, ascending and descending chains and iron buckets which brought rubbish from below to be carted away; or perhaps one morning he found workmen had been kindly shoring up his family abode with huge timbers to make it safer. "A wet week comes, and the gravel in his front garden turns to clay; the tradespeople tread it backwards and forwards to and from the street door; he can hardly get out to business or home to supper without slipping and he strongly objects to a temporary way of wet planks, erected for his use and the use of the passers-by, over a yawning cavern underneath the pavement" . . . but at last, after much labour and many vicissitudes, even the Underground Railway was completed.'

By agreement with the Great Western and Great Northern Railways, whose trains were to have access to the Metropolitan tracks, the railway was laid to the mixed gauge. This means that there were three rails, the outer ones giving the Great Western broad gauge of 7 ft. $0\frac{1}{4}$ in. and the platform-side rail and inside rail giving the standard gauge of 4 ft. $8\frac{1}{2}$ in. favoured by the Great Northern (and, indeed, by almost every British railway except the Great Western). The use of the broad gauge meant that the trench, or, in engineering parlance, 'covered way', for the Metropolitan had to be 28 ft. 6 in. wide. Later extensions, where only the 4 ft. $8\frac{1}{2}$ in. gauge was used, were only 25 ft. wide. A typical section of the original covered way shows an elliptical brick arch of 28 ft. 6 in. span, with the arch springing from side walls resting on 4 ft. wide footings well below rail level. There was no concrete foundation for the side walls, and there was no invert to the covered way; i.e., if the structure is imagined to represent the sides and top of a box, the box had no bottom. In some later parts of the covered way an invert of brick or concrete was provided, and on other sections they have been added later. Beneath the centre of the covered way, under the space between the tracks (the 'six-foot' way), ran an 18-in. diameter drain.

In places where there was not enough depth above the railway to build a brick arch, cast-iron girders (sometimes wrought iron) were used to span the tracks. On the original section of the work, the ground was dug out to the full width of 33 ft. 6 in. (allowing for the brickwork) and to the full depth, the sides being supported by timber while the brickwork was built. In later sections of London covered way (for the District Railway) the practice was to dig 6 ft. wide trenches for the side walls and build these walls up to a height of about 10 ft. from the bottom of the trench. The excavation was then carried down across the full width of the railway to the top of the new walls and the arch was built from side wall to side wall. The remaining spoil inside the new covered way was not taken out until this had been done, and if necessary, the surface restored. This method caused less disturbance to the soil on each side of the line and this reduced subsidence or cracking in neighbouring buildings, the cost of repairing which could be very high and had to be met by the railway. Sir Edward Watkin, one of the best-known chairmen of the Metropolitan Railway Company, told shareholders that work on the repair of a single London chapel, the fabric of which had been cracked during an extension to the railway, cost £14,500. This was at a time when the construction of the covered way for the railway itself, including brickwork, drains, etc., cost only £40–£50 a yard.

With modern methods and materials substituted for the old, the 'cut-and-cover' method is still the one used for most of the world's underground railways. In most places it costs the least to build, and as the stations are only just below ground level passengers can reach the platform quickly by stairways or inclined ramps. Unless the railway can follow existing streets, however, or be run through an area not yet built up or due for demolition and redevelopment, a great deal of expensive disturbance to property is involved which makes the cost prohibitive. Deep tunnels down beneath the foundations of buildings are then the answer; we shall come to those presently.

The Clerkenwell tunnel, already mentioned, was built between November 1860 and May 1862. The depth from the surface to rail level varies between 29 ft. and 59 ft. It was near this tunnel that the Fleet River, then carried in a lightly-built brick sewer, 10 ft. in diameter and resting on rubble in the old river bed, burst through the retaining wall in June 1862, and flooded the workings to a depth of 10 ft. in some places. This was the only serious accident attending the whole of the original works.

The intention at first was to make the stations completely underground, and Baker Street, Portland Road (renamed Great Portland Street in 1917), and Gower Street (renamed Euston Square in 1909) were so constructed. The platforms at the original stations were about 10 ft. wide, but the width was increased in later years when the broad gauge tracks were removed.

The Farringdon terminus was built on the site of the City Cattle Market, which, as mentioned previously, had been removed to Islington. The Great Western and Metropolitan between them leased the basement of the new central meat market at Smithfield for use as a goods depot.

A great deal of thought had been given to the way in which the line would be worked. There were doubts about ventilation if steam locomotives were used; some suggested cable traction and others the atmospheric system. Neither of these ideas found favour – which was probably just as well.

In giving evidence before the Parliamentary Committee of 1854, Fowler, who had thought a great deal about propulsion methods, stated that he would use an ordinary locomotive but would dispense with the fire. By using a 'plain cylindrical, egg-ended boiler', which would be charged at each end of the line with water and steam at high pressure, his locomotive would be able to complete a single trip easily. By experiment, he found that even an ordinary locomotive, without modification, would haul a train the length of the line without a fire, provided it had a full head of steam to start with. (Sir Daniel Gooch tried the same thing with the same results.) I. K. Brunel, of the Great Western Railway, supported Fowler before the committee, but he also said that he did not see why an ordinary locomotive, with a fire in the firebox, could not be used. 'I thought', he said, 'the impression had been exploded long since that railway tunnels required much ventilation'. (It must be remembered, in considering this, that all the experts agreed at the time that 20-ton trains would be enough to carry the traffic. In fact, 120-ton trains hauled by 45-ton locomotives proved to be needed, so that ventilation had to be improved.)

Fowler went ahead with plans for his fireless locomotive, and Robert Stephenson & Co., of Newcastle, were asked, late in 1860, to build a prototype. It had, in fact, a small firebox, but there was a large mass of firebrick in a chamber in the boiler barrel proper. The idea was to run the locomotive in the ordinary way on open sections of line, getting the firebricks really hot, and then damp down the fire in the covered section, the firebricks acting as a heat reservoir. This locomotive was a 2–4–0 tender engine with four 5 ft. 6 in. coupled wheels and cylinders 15 in. in diameter with 24-in. stroke. Exhaust steam from the cylinders was not allowed to escape into the tunnels but was turned into an injection condenser fitted with an air pump. The locomotive weighed 32 tons and the tender 14 tons, both in full working order with fuel and water. It cost £4,500.

In October 1861 the engine was taken out on the Great Western Railway. It ran for 7½ miles as an ordinary locomotive and then was turned to run back. The fire was shut off by dampers and the exhaust steam was turned into the condensing tanks. Unfortunately, in 12 minutes the condensing apparatus was so hot that steam was coming out of the air pump delivery pipe mixed with boiling water. In the same period, the boiler pressure fell from 120 lb. per sq. in. to 80 lb. and the firebricks, which had been at 'a clear white heat', were almost black in appearance. The water from the condenser seems also to have formed the boiler feed, so that the failure of this apparatus meant that the boiler was rapidly running dry. The fire was dropped, but the heat from the firebricks could still have caused a boiler explosion.

It has long been supposed that this was the end of what came to be known as 'Fowler's Ghost', but the *Engineer* of 16 August 1895 spoke of a further trial – also unsatisfactory – in the tunnels between King's Cross and Edgware Road, and a photograph of what seems to be this occasion is reproduced in this book. A comparison of photographs brought to light in 1963 shows that it might have been the 'Ghost' which propelled the open wagons used by the inspection party on 24 May 1862 (see Plate 3). The locomotive was ultimately sold to Mr. Isaac Watt Boulton. In this we are lucky, for in 1927 Alfred Rosling

Bennett wrote a book called *The Chronicles of Boulton's Siding*, in which we learn of the 'Ghost' at Boulton's where it arrived, packed in seven wagons, on 9 October 1865. The size of the driving wheels, as measured on arrival, was 5 ft. 6 in. and not as Sir Benjamin Baker's paper on the Metropolitan (to the Institution of Civil Engineers in 1885) had said, 6 ft. The workmanship of the unusual locomotive was said to be superb. Boulton proposed to turn the 'Ghost' into a standard-gauge saddle tank, and the work of conversion was in hand when the firm went out of business. The 'Ghost' was sold to Beyer, Peacock & Co. and vanished into the scrap yard.

In 1922, Robert Stephenson & Co., of Darlington, found in their records a drawing which is clearly of 'Fowler's Ghost'. It agrees well with the description given by Sir Benjamin Baker in his paper, except for the size of the driving wheels, which were as described by Boulton. The firm also found that a letter with a tracing of a proposed bogie tank engine had been sent to Fowler on 18 December 1861, two months after the trial trip on the Great Western. Later, an actual drawing of this locomotive was discovered. It would have been similar in many ways to the 'Ghost', including the firebricks, but would have been without air pumps. It would have been a 4–2–2, and its strangest feature, perhaps, was that the boiler capacity would have been increased by mounting a second boiler barrel on top of the first. The whole twin-barrel arrangement would have been covered by a great saddle tank. The locomotive would have worked at the very high boiler pressure, for those days, of 200 lb. per sq. in. This interesting design did not get beyond the paper stage. The drawings are reproduced in A. R. Bennett's book.

Daniel Gooch, locomotive superintendent of the Great Western, was eventually asked to design a locomotive for the Metropolitan. He decided on a 2–4–0 tank design with 6 ft. coupled wheels and outside cylinders 16 in. by 24 in. The heating surface of the firebox was 125 sq. ft. and of the tubes 615 sq. ft. The grate area was 18.5 sq. ft. As well as the normal feed tank holding 375 gallons of water, there was a special condensing tank holding 420 gallons. On trial in October 1862 the engine ran with a 36-ton train from Farringdon Street to Paddington in 20 minutes. The locomotive itself weighed 38 tons.

With these Great Western locomotives and Great Western eight-wheel carriages of a type known as 'Long Charleys', the service was prepared by Myles (afterwards Sir Myles) Fenton, the Metropolitan's operating superintendent. The long coaches were very comfortable for their day and had a very large capacity. All 49 were fitted with gas lighting.

These coaches were not used by the inspection party of shareholders on 30 August 1862, when they travelled, largely in the contractor's open wagons, to see what their money was producing. On an earlier trip, on 24 May 1862, were Mr. and Mrs. Gladstone, and a well-known photograph shows them sitting in state in a wagon, attended by Mr. Fowler. The same wagon held a large number of other notable personages, as can be seen from the reproduction in this book. The two wagons seem to have been pushed by the locomotive.

At last the line was ready for inspection, and in December 1862 it passed, except for a few minor points, the scrutiny of the Inspecting Officer of the Board of Trade. The final inspection by Colonel Yolland took place on 3 January 1863, and rehearsals of the full traffic were carried on from 4 January to 8 January. There had been a delay caused mainly by difficulties with the block signalling apparatus. The disc block instruments used were devised by C. E. Spagnoletti, telegraph superintendent of the Great Western.

The service started running on Saturday, 10 January 1863, with the immediate success already noted; the event had been celebrated the day before with a great banquet for 350 guests at Farringdon Street. All the stations were decorated.

Workmen's trains were a particular interest of Pearson's; though he did not live to see the Metropolitan work them – he died on 14 September 1862 – he must have known that at last they were coming. The Metropolitan was the first London railway to issue workmen's tickets, in May 1864, though others soon followed.

It soon became evident that the service provided by the Great Western, whose main interest was in through trains, was not good enough for the amount of short-distance traffic offering. Also, nothing had been done about freight trains, although the connection with the Great Northern was nearly ready to be opened. The Great Western steadily drew away from the Metropolitan, which with equal determination was drawing away from the Great Western. The mutual dislike was intensified by the fact that Charles Saunders, secretary of the Great Western, had brushed – hard – against John Parson, now the Metropolitan's deputy chairman, over the Oxford, Worcester & Wolverhampton Railway's affairs.

This animosity culminated in a letter from Saunders to the effect that the Great Western would not work the Metropolitan Line after

30 September. This failed to produce the expected panic, and a second letter was sent advancing the date to 11 August. To make sure that the Metropolitan was properly brought to heel, the Great Western, knowing that the Metropolitan had neither locomotives nor coaches of its own, made it clear that it would not sell the rolling stock then working the line to the Metropolitan. The answer of the Metropolitan was to hire locomotives and stock from the Great Northern (some rolling stock also from the L.N.W.R.) until its own equipment was ready. There were difficulties, of course. The train service had to be reduced, and the Great Northern 0–4–2 and 0–6–0 tender locomotives were not ideal for the work, but the line kept going until at last its own coaches, built by the Ashbury Railway Carriage & Iron Company, of Manchester, and its own locomotives, designed by Fowler and Beyer, Peacock & Co. Ltd., of Manchester, and built by Beyer, Peacock, arrived on the scene.

The coaches, based on the Great Western model but adapted to the narrower gauge, were said to be a great improvement on anything used on the line before and better than many main-line coaches of the era, and the locomotives were certainly better than the rather strange assortment provided by the Great Northern, though these saved the day for the Metropolitan.

The new locomotives were 4–4–0 tank engines with outside cylinders. The coupled wheels were 5 ft. 9 in. and the leading wheels 3 ft. in diameter. The tube heating surface was 841 sq. ft., that of the firebox 101.6 sq. ft., and the grate 19 sq. ft. The boiler pressure was 120 lb., but this was raised to 160 lb. in later locomotives. The cylinders had a diameter of 17¼ in. and the stroke was 24 in. The weight, with 1,170 gallons of water in the tanks, was 45 tons. Tractive effort at 80 per cent boiler pressure was 13,100 lb.

The first batch of 18 of these locomotives bore classical names as follows:

1	*Jupiter*	7	*Orion*	13	*Daphne*
2	*Mars*	8	*Pluto*	14	*Dido*
3	*Juno*	9	*Minerva*	15	*Aurora*
4	*Mercury*	10	*Cerberus*	16	*Achilles*
5	*Apollo*	11	*Latona*	17	*Ixion*
6	*Medusa*	12	*Cyclops*	18	*Hercules*

All the nameplates were eventually removed.

The Fowler locomotives were so successful that they remained, with a few modifications, the motive power of the tunnel lines until electrification. The first were known as the 'A' type, but the 'B' type were very similar. Between them, they eventually numbered 66. When the District came to need its own motive power, it brought engines of the same type from the same builders and this added another 54 to their numbers. One of the 'A' class (No. 23) is now preserved in the London Transport Museum at Covent Garden. The fuel at first was coke made from the finest Durham coal, but this was superseded after six years by South Wales semi-anthracite coal.

When the railway started its public service there were outcries about poor ventilation, and a fan had to be provided at what was then Portland Road station. At other stations glass was removed from windows. Later, portions of the covered way were opened up to improve ventilation still further, and in 1871–2 'blow-holes' (an idea of Pearson's originally) were made in the tunnel roof to the road above on the section between Edgware Road and King's Cross. The sudden eruption of air, steam, and smoke from these holes as a train passed below was said to have been very disturbing to horses in the roadway above.

This experience led to stations on extensions and on the District Railway being built as far as possible in the open with a cutting at each end. There was also, where possible, an intermediate open section between stations.

Meanwhile, Fowler had been busy building another railway, the Hammersmith & City. This was built by a separate company with the backing of the Great Western and the Metropolitan and was conceived as a feeder to the Metropolitan line. The new line ran from the Great Western main line about a mile out of Paddington and described a quarter of a circle round the suburbs of the day to end pointing almost south at Hammersmith. There were intermediate stations at Notting Hill (now Ladbroke Grove) and at Shepherd's Bush (not the present station). A branch left the main line at Latimer Road (the station of that name did not open until 16 December 1868) and ran to Kensington (Addison Road – now Olympia). The main line opened on 13 June 1864 and the branch on 1 July the same year. The 'branch' was in fact a connecting line with the West London and the West London Extension Railway, which gave a route from Paddington via West Brompton and over the Thames to Battersea and the south, including a connection with Victoria. This later resulted in such curiosities as the London, Brighton & South Coast running trains to Brighton from Paddington and broad-gauge Great

Western trains working regularly to Victoria (on the London, Chatham & Dover side). The Hammersmith & City became a joint responsibility of the Great Western and Metropolitan on 1 July 1867. At the start, the line was worked by the Great Western, but as the relations between the companies improved again, Metropolitan trains started running through to Hammersmith on 1 April 1865. The track was mixed gauge. Because of delays to trains on the section of Great Western main line, two extra tracks were put down for the Hammersmith & City, the work being finished in May 1867.

So much for the western side of London. Farther east, the Great Northern had started running through trains to Farringdon Street on 1 October 1863, and on the same day the Great Western started running broad-gauge trains between Farringdon and Windsor, though the service was withdrawn at the end of the year. In the next month the Metropolitan let the contract for an eastwards extension to Moorgate Street. Powers for this had been obtained in 1861, and the preliminary matters had been taken care of while the earlier part of the line was still being built. The contractor, John Kelk, started work early the next year, but in the meantime a further decision had been made. To keep the Great Northern trains clear of the Metropolitan's and give them proper access to the goods depot and meat market at Smithfield two extra tracks would be laid on the Moorgate extension, and the existing lines would be quadrupled all the way back to King's Cross. This was an undertaking of some magnitude, because it meant building another double-track tunnel at the side of the long Clerkenwell tunnel. The work was authorized in 1864 and also went to John Kelk. Fowler, of course, was the engineer. The 'Widened Lines', as they have always been called, run north of the Metropolitan tracks from King's Cross to the 'new' Clerkenwell tunnel. Built between November 1865 and May 1867, the tunnel is 733 yds. in length. At its eastern end the mouth is some 16 ft. lower than that of the original tunnel, and the Widened Lines dip under the Metropolitan tracks and run from there to Moorgate on the south side of the other lines. The Metropolitan lines were carried across the Widened Lines by an unusual wrought-iron bridge which also acted at a strut between the walls of the deep cutting. The bridge was well known in railway circles as the 'Ray Street Gridiron'. It was replaced by a concrete raft in 1960, but the girders of the original bridge had already been renewed in 1892.

A new station was built at Farringdon Street for the extension, and the line was open from that station to Moorgate by 23 December 1865. The Widened Lines were opened from Farringdon to Aldersgate Street on 1 March 1866 and to Moorgate on 1 July of the same year. The new Clerkenwell tunnel held up the Farringdon–King's Cross opening until 17 February 1868. Meanwhile, the London, Chatham & Dover had been building towards Ludgate Hill and Snow Hill. This line met a short spur from the Metropolitan at West Street Junction, just north of Farringdon, and a new cross-London route was made available on 1 January 1866. The Widened Lines were used by passenger trains from the date the King's Cross–Farringdon section was opened. The Smithfield market, for the traffic of which so much preparation had been made, was officially opened in November 1868, but not served by trains until 3 May 1869. A connection had also been made between the newly built Midland Railway line to London and the Metropolitan. This was opened on 13 July 1868 and carried local trains from Bedford into Moorgate. As St. Pancras was not to be opened for another 2½ months, Moorgate was in fact the Midland's first London terminus.

The Great Western broad-gauge trains had been projected from Farringdon to Aldersgate and then to Moorgate over the new Widened Lines when they were opened – they were mixed-gauge lines. In August 1868, however, it was agreed that the broad-gauge passenger trains should be withdrawn from the Metropolitan, and the last train on the 7 ft. gauge left Moorgate on 15 March 1869. Great Western goods trains ran to Smithfield on the standard gauge (the last freight train ran to Smithfield on 28 July 1962).

Before we leave this area, it is worth noting that in 1871 a connection from Snow Hill to the Widened Lines in the Moorgate direction was opened – the earlier ones faced King's Cross. London, Chatham & Dover trains reached Moorgate by this route from 1 September 1871, and they continued to use the route until 1 April 1916. The line was still open, in theory, until 1927, although by then much of the track had gone from the tunnel. The tunnel was demolished in the general clearance of the site of the Smithfield Poultry Market, burnt down in January 1958.

Another Metropolitan move towards expansion, small in itself, was to have much significance later on in the railway's history. In 1864, the Metropolitan & St. John's Wood Railway was incorporated, with Fowler as engineer. This was to run from Baker Street to meet the Hampstead Junction Railway near the latter's Finchley Road station. In fact, the line got into financial difficulties and finished up – and then only with the help of the Metropolitan – as a single-track line which left the Metropolitan by a junction at Baker Street and ended at Swiss Cottage. It was opened on 13 April 1868. When, in the following year, the St. John's Wood proposed to increase its through services over the Metropolitan line to six trains an hour instead of three, the Metropolitan closed the junction, refused to allow through trains, and made passengers walk to the Metropolitan platform at Baker Street.

II The Metropolitan District and the Inner Circle

THE METROPOLITAN was not alone in wanting expansion of the London lines. So many promoters came along with schemes that a Select Committee of the House of Lords was set up in 1863, and a joint committee of both Houses in 1864, to sort out the tangled mass of applications before Parliament. The 1863 committee wanted all the main-line termini linked by rail and suggested that the best way would be to extend the Metropolitan at both ends and form an 'inner circuit' by a new line linking the ends of the Metropolitan but running nearer the Thames. For many years there had been agitation for an embankment on the north side of the Thames which could be used as a new through road to reduce the congestion in the traffic-choked Strand. It was also wanted as the route for a new trunk sewer. Despite some Londoners' remarks about the early Metropolitan, it is to be hoped that it was not the agitation of the Metropolitan Board of Works for a sewer route which gave Fowler the idea of building the southern link line under the Embankment.

Fowler first put forward a line from Farringdon to Blackfriars and then to a Westminster terminus under the new embankment road, powers for which had been granted in 1862. Another new line would run from Paddington to Notting Hill and then, through Kensington Gardens, back to Westminster to meet his other proposed line. Before powers could be sought for this route, the House of Lords had changed its mind and wanted a line to run east from Moorgate to Tower Hill and then to turn to Cannon Street and Blackfriars – a much more expensive route than Fowler's.

The Metropolitan did its best. It applied for powers to build from Moorgate to Trinity Square (Tower Hill), and separately, from Paddington to Notting Hill Gate, Kensington, and Brompton. These two applications were both granted, the enabling Acts – the Metropolitan Railway (Notting Hill and Brompton Extension) Act and the Metropolitan Railway (Tower Hill Extension) Act – both receiving the Royal Assent on 29 July 1864.

The intermediate section needed to complete the 'inner circuit' – from South Kensington (Brompton) to Tower Hill – was handed to a new company. This was the Metropolitan District Railway Company, also incorporated by an Act of 29 July 1864, making its first appearance on the London scene. Its name came from the title that Fowler had given his inner circuit plans, 'Metropolitan District Railways', and the Metropolitan's chairman, W. A. Wilkinson, and three other Metropolitan directors were on the board. The engineer-in-chief was Fowler, and the chosen contractors were Peto & Betts, Kelk, and Waring Bros. It was clear that the Metropolitan District, as a company, was a device for splitting the effort of raising capital for the work. It was expected that the two companies would amalgamate as soon as possible, and the terms of amalgamation were actually drawn up for use when required. It did not work out like that!

As well as the 'circle completion' section, the new company had powers to build alongside the Metropolitan from South Kensington to Gloucester Road and continue through Earl's Court to a junction with the West London Extension Railway at West Brompton, and to build a line from Kensington High Street, also through Earl's Court, to join the West London Railway near Addison Road. Work started at Kensington on 29 June 1865 and at several other points simultaneously, and the northern section of the circle was under way.

The Metropolitan, having taken a look at the cost of its City extension, started at the other end on the extension from Paddington. Fowler's original idea had been to build this in easy territory through Kensington Gardens and Hyde Park, but the opposition was too strong and the present route was selected instead. It entailed cuttings 42 ft. deep and a 421-yd. tunnel at Campden Hill as well as considerable sums in compensation to property owners. In Leinster Gardens, where the railway runs under the road, the railway had to rebuild the façade of two houses, Nos. 23 and 24, which are just false fronts, to act as screens for the line. They have figured in many stories and, no doubt, in many practical jokes. The line was opened to Gloucester Road on 1 October 1868 and to South Kensington on 24 December of the same year.

The District had its difficulties because of the built-up nature of the land through which its covered way was being cut. It also met London's rivers just as the Metropolitan had done to the north. The West Bourne, constricted and fouled and renamed the Ranelagh sewer, had to be carried in a 29-yd. conduit over the station at Sloane Square. The District found itself mixed up with the widening of Tothill Street and a slum clearance scheme near the present London Transport headquarters; it had to take special precautions for nearly 100 yd. as it passed by Westminster Abbey; and at the end there was a frantic rush in which 3,000 men worked day and night to get the line open to Westminster Bridge in time for the Christmas traffic of 1868. They just did it, the line being opened from South Kensington to Westminster Bridge on Christmas Eve.

The trains and motive power were supplied by the Metropolitan, running on from South Kensington. There were three intermediate stations, as there still are – Sloane Square, Victoria, and St. James's Park. Westminster station, from 1870, had a subway to the nearby Houses of Parliament. In 1871 Mr. Gladstone is reported to have said: 'The convenience of the line had an influence of remarkable efficiency in removing the members of the House of Commons from their seats at a certain hour of the evening'. On his death in 1898 Mr. Gladstone's body was carried at midnight through this subway for the lying-in-state in Westminster Hall.

On 12 April 1869 the line to West Brompton, where there was a station next to that of the West London Extension Railway, was opened. It was worked by a shuttle service from Gloucester Road. The District tracks between South Kensington and Gloucester Road were ready but not used, at any rate not regularly, until the line was also open to Blackfriars and there was a through service from that station to West Brompton.

The line from Kensington High Street to the West London Railway was ready by the autumn of 1869 and, after some thought of building its own station, the District made arrangements to use the West London's existing Addison Road station, but regular traffic did not begin until 1872.

The District now ran into money troubles and wanted work on the

Embankment, with which its own works were inextricably mixed, to be held up until the South Kensington–Westminster section was bringing in some money. The Metropolitan Board of Works, on the other hand, wanted to get its sewer working and the embankment completed. The impasse remained until, in 1869, authority was given by Parliament to issue preference stock for the remaining money required. The railway could then proceed, and although it had to be re-excavated from the filling behind the completed embankment wall it was opened to Blackfriars on 30 May 1870, with intermediate stations at Charing Cross and the Temple. As far as possible, stations were in open cuttings with vertical retaining walls. The platforms were 300 ft. long and the elliptical arched iron roofs had a 50 ft. 6 in. span. At Temple station a special flat form of roof had to be built because an agreement between the railway and the Duke of Norfolk, whose property the line crossed here, stipulated that this station should not have a raised roof.

The remaining section of the line from Blackfriars to Mansion House was opened formally on 1 July 1871, and to public traffic two days later on Monday, 3 July. In the same month the District opened its own station in South Kensington, which it had built, together with a stretch of track, to avoid using the Metropolitan's facilities.

The last apparently childish move arose from an argument between the District and the Metropolitan. The Metropolitan had worked the services for 55 per cent of the gross receipts. Any extra trains had to be paid for out of the District's percentage, and as it always wanted more trains its actual receipts fell to about two-fifths of the total. The District decided that the only thing to do was to run its own trains and gave the necessary notice to the Metropolitan. The notice was due to expire on 1 July 1871.

In the meantime, the Metropolitan directors who were also on the board of the District had resigned and a new director had been brought in. He was James Staats Forbes, who had trained under Saunders on the Great Western, been general manager of a railway in the Netherlands, and was now general manager of the London, Chatham & Dover. He became chairman of the District in November 1872.

When Mansion House station opened, the District worked its own lines and also half of the trains from Mansion House to Moorgate. It purchased its own rolling stock and built a depot for it at what is now called Lillie Bridge. The agreement as to which railway should work which trains was concluded only at the last moment, less than a week before the District was due to assume complete independence. To make matters worse, after a very critical report on the Metropolitan's affairs, the Metropolitan shareholders forced the Board on 7 August 1872, to accept Sir Edward Watkin as chairman, and John Parson had to resign from the board to make room for him. Watkin was already chairman of the Manchester, Sheffield & Lincolnshire and of the South Eastern Railway. In his latter capacity he was already at daggers drawn with Forbes, and the situation was not improved when, in 1873, Forbes became chairman as well as general manager of the London, Chatham & Dover.

But we are anticipating. When the District achieved independence it found that this was not an automatic passport to success. Results were disappointing, and the company's stock fell so low that there was talk of amalgamation with the Metropolitan. There was still expansion in the air, for all that. An Act was obtained in 1872 to build a line from Earl's Court to join the London & South Western at Barnes, and in the following year an independent company, known as the Hammersmith Extension Railway Company, was given powers to build a line from Earl's Court to Hammersmith Broadway. The independent company was a creation of the District's, which doubted whether it could raise the money under its own name. The line was built and opened quietly on 9 September 1874. The L.S.W.R. agreed to give the District running powers from Hammersmith to Richmond as long as it promised that this should be the only route used to connect its lines with Kew, Richmond, and Barnes. The necessary agreement made, the District was able to scrap its own scheme for an independent line to Barnes. Instead, the District received powers to build the 'Metropolitan District Richmond Extension Railway' (separate capital again) to connect Hammersmith Broadway with the L.S.W.R. lines at Studland Road Junction, near what is now Ravenscourt Park station but which before 1888 was Shaftesbury Road. The Midland Railway took a financial interest in this, as it saw the possibilities of the line in carrying its goods trains between Acton and Kensington.

The Hammersmith Junction line was opened on 1 June 1877, and the District's trains began to work through from Mansion House to Richmond. Encouraged, the District made further use of its running powers by obtaining permission to build a line from Turnham Green to Ealing Broadway, and this was opened on 1 July 1879. In 1883 it made an agreement with the Great Western whereby a short connecting line was put in between the District and the G.W.R. just east of Ealing Broadway. By this line District trains worked from Mansion House to Windsor for about 2½ years, but the service did not pay.

Another extension, opened on 1 March 1880, was the so-called Fulham extension to Putney Bridge from West Brompton. There was a good deal of muddle over what was to happen farther south. At the first there was a scheme which would have taken District trains to Surbiton and L.S.W.R. trains to South Kensington, but eventually the L.S.W.R. decided on a Putney–Wimbledon line instead. This was to be built by a separate company, but powers were obtained by an Act of 1886 to transfer the powers to the L.S.W.R. In due course, the line was built from Putney Bridge to Wimbledon by the L.S.W.R. It included a trellis girder bridge over the Thames which had a public footbridge on one side of it. The District service began on 3 June 1889, and the L.S.W.R. working from East Putney to Wimbledon started on 1 July. The East Putney–Putney Bridge section, which included the bridge itself, was used only by District trains.

Before we leave the District's 'west country', it is worth noting that for a time it worked, for 50 per cent of receipts, a locally-promoted line from Mill Hill Park (renamed Acton Town on 1 March 1910) to the old Hounslow Town station, on a spur from Osterley. The authorized line should have gone to Hounslow Barracks, but the spur was opened first, two months before the Enabling Act for it received the Royal Assent. Through trains worked from Hounslow Town to Mansion House for a few months after the opening on 1 May 1883, but in December they were cut back to Earl's Court. When Hounslow Barracks station was opened on 21 July 1884 it was served by a shuttle service from Osterley. On 31 March 1886 Hounslow Town was closed, being replaced the next day by Heston Hounslow on the main line, when a through service started to run between Mill Hill Park and Hounslow Barracks. Hounslow Town station was, however, to come to life again in 1903.

On the east side of London there was no such picture. The shortage of money for the more expensive construction in the City was acute, and neither the Metropolitan nor the District made a move. The Metropolitan had served notices to purchase on the owners of property east of Moorgate in 1865, but nothing was done except that the railway managed, in 1869, to get an extension of time. The powers granted to the District, which had no extension of time, lapsed in 1870. It looked as though the Circle would never be completed.

When the Liverpool Street terminus of the Great Eastern was being built, the Metropolitan managed to extend its lines to join the Great Eastern's. At one time, after the connection had been made in 1875, trains from Hammersmith ran right into the main-line station. The Metropolitan was continued to Aldgate the next year, but this may have been something of a forced move, as City interests, tired of waiting for the two railway companies, had formed a Metropolitan Inner Circle Completion Railway Company in 1874. This company formed some sort of agreement with the District and it issued a prospectus in late 1877. Sir Edward Watkin used all his influence to prevent the money for the line being raised, and he succeeded, but he must have realized that the writing was on the wall and at last he came to what might be called an armed peace with the District.

The Metropolitan and District (City Lines and Extensions) Act of 1879 authorized the two railways to complete the Circle jointly and also to build a line from Aldgate to connect with the East London Railway at Whitechapel. The Act also obliged the two companies to work the Circle line when it was completed. Even now Sir Edward Watkin was determined to be awkward. The Metropolitan hastily built its own line under its own powers to Tower Hill and built a station of sorts there at high speed, opening it on 25 September 1882. Its actual value may be judged from the fact that it was abandoned two years later (though the ticket hall survived – as a tea warehouse – until 1940) but this line caused a lot of trouble when it was taken over by the joint Metropolitan/District undertaking and compensation had to be discussed. Objections of various sorts were also brought up by the South Eastern, of which, as we know, Watkin was also chairman.

Despite all this, Sir John Hawkshaw and J. Wolfe Barry, the engineers, finished the Circle and it was opened on 6 October 1884. In the meantime, the District had built an independent terminus at Whitechapel and some of its trains terminated there. The Metropolitan ran from Hammersmith (Hammersmith & City) via the northern half of the Circle and thence over the East London Railway to New Cross (South Eastern). The District through trains ran from Hammersmith also (District station) over the southern side of the Circle and then on to the East London to New Cross (London, Brighton & South Coast). There were both north and south curves at Aldgate; that from the northern side of the Circle was purely Metropolitan property.

Although the lines were now operating, there was constant bickering between the two companies. One frequent source of trouble was the division of receipts on the Circle, each company trying to claim as much traffic for itself as possible. This was aggravated in 1884 by an astute move on the part of the District. The original authorization for the District did not include a direct connection between Kensington High Street and Gloucester Road. The Metropolitan had such a line and opposed one for the District. In 1870, however, without Parliamentary authority, the District built such a line and the Metropolitan agreed to its use as a relief line. It was little used until 1884, when the District diverted its Circle Line trains over it and claimed it as part of the Circle. By doing this it was able to claim a higher percentage of receipts because it was making, it claimed, more use of its own lines and less of the Metropolitan's. The matter went to the Courts, and it took until 1903 for the courts to rule that the 'Cromwell Curve', as it was known, was not part of the Inner Circle. The final condemnation of this practice, which had continued for only five weeks or so, took nearly 19 years.

Other milestones before the end of the century included the resignation in 1894 of Watkin from the Metropolitan after a stroke and his replacement by the more amenable John Bell as chairman, so that relations at last improved; the passing of an Act in 1897 allowing the District to build a deep-level 'electric express' tube line under its existing tracks between Earl's Court and Mansion House, with one intermediate station at Charing Cross; and the consideration of electrification for the whole line.

There were also Middle and Outer Circles, though neither was ever a complete ring. The Outer Circle, worked by the London & North Western, was from Broad Street (North London Railway) to Camden Town, Willesden, and the West London Railway, Addison Road, and Mansion House. The Middle Circle was worked by the Great Western, running from Moorgate via the Metropolitan and the Hammersmith & City to Latimer Road and then through Addison Road to the District and Mansion House. These services faded away to nothing in the course of time, leaving only the exhibition services between Olympia and Earl's Court.

III Manchester to Dover via Baker Street

SO FAR WE have seen the Metropolitan under Watkin as a disgruntled parent doing its best to obstruct and control an upstart child, the District, which persisted in kicking over the traces. This is a long way from being the whole picture; probably Watkin considered it not much more than an irritating sideline. He had his mind on bigger things.

It will be recalled that there was a short single line, the St. John's Wood, running north-west for nearly two miles to Swiss Cottage from a junction with the Metropolitan at Baker Street. This line had double track at the two intermediate stations, St. John's Wood and Marlborough Road, and was complete to within a very short distance of the North London's Finchley Road station. It had been opened, as already described, on 13 April 1868.

Sir Edward Watkin appeared on the Metropolitan scene in 1872, and in 1873 the St. John's Wood line obtained powers to extend to Kingsbury (now known as Neasden). The reason for this, Watkin explained later, was two-fold. The works at Edgware Road were to be moved out into the country and the Metropolitan was to break through 'the iron barrier which the skill and acuteness of the larger railway companies had constructed' around it. They wanted to cross the Midland and the North Western lines so that, if an extension was called for at any time, it would go to the Metropolitan and not to the others.

The idea of the other railways building an iron curtain to contain the small and very urban Metropolitan seems slightly comical now, but to a man with Watkin's vision it probably seemed serious enough. He was a main-line man, and he looked on the Metropolitan as a potential main-line railway. On this particular occasion he was asking the shareholders to approve a proposal to carry the St. John's Wood line on to Harrow, and he tempted them by speaking of 'disjointed pieces of railway which will hereafter help to connect your great terminus with Northampton and Birmingham and many other important towns'. The shareholders must have had their field of vision suddenly enlarged. They had put their money in a small, busy, London railway; here was the chairman talking in familiar terms of the Midlands.

The extension was put in hand. On 30 June 1879, the St. John's Wood line was open to West Hampstead; it was doubled from Baker Street on 10 July 1882, the new track running in a separate tunnel alongside the old. On 24 November 1879 it was opened to Willesden Green and on 2 August 1880 to Harrow-on-the-Hill, powers having been granted for this in an Act of 1874. The Metropolitan, through its St. John's Wood company, had now reached out 9½ miles from Baker Street. Among many proposals for building new links and joining existing lines at this period was one, in which Watkin had a hand, for making a new route from the Midlands which would enter London via the Metropolitan. This plan eventually reached Parliament as the Buckinghamshire & Northamptonshire Railways Union Bill, but it was rejected.

Although the Metropolitan was granted powers in 1880 to build on to Rickmansworth and in the following year to Aylesbury, Pinner was not reached until 25 May 1885 and Rickmansworth on 1 September 1887. The Metropolitan, which by now had taken over the St. John's Wood line completely, had its railhead 17½ miles from Baker Street. Meanwhile, in 1886, Watkin was accused at a general meeting of concealing the real reason for this advance to the north-west. Watkin dismissed the implication as a 'phantom of the imagination', having conveniently forgotten his promises of 1874 about the future of the Metropolitan's 'great terminus'.

Nevertheless, although the Metropolitan could not at once raise the money to go on to Aylesbury, it did continue to Chesham. The main line from Rickmansworth to Amersham and north-westwards to Aylesbury was authorized by the Aylesbury & Rickmansworth Railway Act of 1881, and the Chesham branch by the Metropolitan Railway Act of 1885, which empowered the Metropolitan to build a branch railway 2½ miles long from the point where it diverges from the main line, some three-quarters of a mile from Chalfont & Latimer station.

Most of the land for the new sections of railway was purchased at the time from the Duke of Bedford and Lord Chesham, but the land for the final half-mile of the Chesham branch was presented to the railway by the inhabitants to ensure that a station could be built

PLATE 1. Page of drawings from a contemporary journal showing the Metropolitan Railway's stations as originally built

PLATE 2. 'Fowler's Ghost' on a trial run. This photograph was taken near Edgware Road and shows the clean lines of this unusual engine

PLATE 3. An official party, including Mr. Gladstone and Mr. Fowler inspecting the Metropolitan works on 24 May 1862. They travelled in the contractor's wagons

1. Lady Constance Grosvenor. 2. The Duke of Sutherland. 3. Mrs. Gladstone. 4. Mr. T. M. Johnson, *Resident Engineer*. 5. Mr. George Knight, *Contractor*. 6. Mr. Charles Gilpin, M.P. 7. Right Hon. Stuart Wortley. 8. Lord Wenlock. 9. Sir Stephen Glynn, Bart. 10. Mr. Charles Wood. 11. Lord Richard Grosvenor, M.P. 12. Lord Macclesfield. 13. Lord Grosvenor. 14. Lord Ronald Gower. 15. Mr. Fowler, *Engineer*. 16. Right Hon. W. E. Gladstone, M.P. 17. Mr. Armstrong, *Contractor's Agent*.

OPENING
OF THE
METROPOLITAN RAILWAY
On SATURDAY, the 10th day of JANUARY, 1863.

TIME TABLE.
ALL TRAINS ARE FIRST, SECOND AND THIRD CLASS.

DOWN TRAINS from FARRINGDON STREET to PADDINGTON.---WEEK DAYS.

UP TRAINS from PADDINGTON to FARRINGDON STREET.---WEEK DAYS.

SUNDAYS.
DOWN TRAINS from FARRINGDON STREET to PADDINGTON.

UP TRAINS from PADDINGTON to FARRINGDON STREET.

PLATE 4. The Metropolitan Railway's first timetable. There was a 15-minute service for most of the day and the 'church break' on Sunday morning

PLATE 5. Typical scene at Aldgate station in steam days (1902)

PLATE 6. Original District Railway electric stock (1903) with District steam locomotive No. 16 (dating from 1871)

PLATE 7. Metropolitan Railway 'G' class 0-6-4T locomotive, built in 1915, with one of the Metropolitan Railway's first electric locomotives. No. 2 was one of 10 camel-back units delivered in 1905–6

PLATE 8. Brill branch train waiting at the level crossing, Wood Siding station, while the guard operates the crossing gates (1934). This early locomotive is now preserved in the London Transport Museum at Covent Garden

PLATE 9. Metropolitan Railway 'K' class 2-6-4T locomotive No. 116 with a six-coach Aylesbury train, including a Pullman car in its final livery

PLATE 10. One of the two Pullman cars which ran on the Metropolitan, 'Galatea', in its original livery at the Birmingham Railway Carriage & Wagon Company's works

PLATE 11. Interior of one of the Metropolitan Pullman cars. There were 19 armchair seats at which refreshments were served

PLATE 12. An Inner Circle train in 1935 made up of stock dating from 1914 and 1921. This type of stock was in use on the Circle Line until 1950

PLATE 13. '*John Hampden*', one of the 20 Metropolitan 1,200-h.p. Bo-Bo electric locomotives delivered in 1922–23, now preserved in the London Transport Museum at Covent Garden

PLATE 14. A train of 'T' stock, backbone of the Metropolitan electric services to Rickmansworth and Watford for over 30 years

PLATE 15. The Metropolitan Railway provided all the services of a main line. This photograph shows parcels vans at Baker Street in the early 1930s

in the centre of Chesham instead of on the outskirts, as was originally intended. The Metropolitan subsequently purchased further strips of land extending almost 1½ miles north of the station in the direction of Berkhamsted.

In May 1889 the double-track railway from Rickmansworth through Chorleywood to Chalfont Road (as Chalfont & Latimer station was known until November 1915) and the single-track branch to Chesham were almost complete; so, in recognition of their generosity, the people of Chesham were invited to inspect the branch on 15 May and were entertained to a banquet. Seven weeks later, on 8 July, the line from Rickmansworth to Chesham was opened to traffic. The main line from Chalfont Road to Amersham and on to Aylesbury was not opened until 1 September 1892; for more than three years Chesham was the northern terminus of the Metropolitan. Even before the line was opened to Chesham, the Metropolitan Railway Company catered for travellers from and to Chesham by running special omnibuses between Chesham (Crown Hotel) and the railhead at Rickmansworth.

The opening of the line to Aylesbury had a significance beyond the fact that the Metropolitan now served the town. From Aylesbury there ran onwards, in the same north-westerly direction as the Metropolitan, the Aylesbury & Buckingham Railway. Opened on 23 September 1868, this ran to Quainton Road and then swung to the north to join the Bletchley–Oxford line of the Buckinghamshire Railway. The junction, which was where the Buckinghamshire Railway's own branch to Buckingham and Banbury left the main line, was called Verney Junction after Sir Harry Verney, chairman of the Buckinghamshire Railway; there was not much else in the locality to call it after.

From the Aylesbury & Buckingham there turned off at Quainton Road a light railway built by the Duke of Buckingham as a private venture. The duke was active in railway affairs and controlled or helped to guide many companies. He was a director of the Buckinghamshire Railway, among others. His private line ran at first to Wotton and was opened on 1 April 1871. The next year it was extended to the foot of Brill Hill. There was a passenger service from January 1872, but the primary purpose of the line was to carry supplies and produce connected with the duke's own estates. It was long known locally as the Wotton Tramway, whatever its official name at the time. It was 6½ miles long and of standard gauge; it was worked for many years by two tiny Aveling & Porter geared locomotives, one of which is preserved in the London Transport Museum.

The Aylesbury & Buckingham was a single-track line, and if it was to be of use to the Metropolitan something had to be done about it. The Metropolitan therefore took it over from 1 July 1891 and started to double it in readiness to connect with the approaching Metropolitan metals. When the link had been achieved, through trains were run to Verney Junction, a station in the middle of nowhere, and the Metropolitan was now just over 50 miles from Baker Street.

In 1883 there was a scheme to build an Oxford, Aylesbury & Metropolitan Junction Railway from Oxford to connect with the Wotton Tramway at Brill, only 10 miles or so away, and continue over the route of the Tramway. The scheme came to nothing, but it was revived as the Oxford & Aylesbury Tramroad in 1888. An Act was duly obtained; but all that happened was that the Wotton Tramway was taken over under the new name in 1894 – no new lines were built. The Oxford & Aylesbury remained the owners of the line, but the Metropolitan worked it until 1933 and the London Passenger Transport Board continued the service until the line closed in 1935. During the Metropolitan days it was called the Brill branch, and it was normally worked by one of the original 'A' class Fowler locomotives, hauling one passenger carriage and such goods wagons as were necessary. At level crossings the driver or fireman got down and opened the gates; a large key, carried on the footplate, was used to unlock any points that had to be changed. There was very little traffic, and it is not surprising that this rural offshoot, reaching out 51 miles from London, was closed as soon as the London Passenger Transport Board, which inherited the line in 1933, could arrange it.

What connection was there between this rural curiosity and the busy line between Paddington and the City? Sir Edward Watkin told the shareholders in 1889 that 'in view of the policy of completing the links required to connect your line at Aylesbury with the systems of railway to the north and east . . . negotiations have been entered into with the South Eastern Company to the south and with the Manchester, Sheffield & Lincolnshire Company to the north, with a view to the development of traffic by existing and future routes. The Great Northern Company will have the opportunity of joining in the proposed Agreement, should they see fit.' The chairman of the South Eastern was, of course, Sir Edward Watkin, and the chairman of the

M.S. & L. was also Sir Edward Watkin. The outposts of his empire were being linked at last.

In 1890 Watkins showed the Metropolitan's shareholders a great map on which the trunk route over his three lines was displayed for all to see. The shareholders were invited to give the Manchester, Sheffield & Lincolnshire running powers over the Metropolitan from Quainton Road to Baker Street on the basis of one-third receipts going to the M.S. & L. and the other two-thirds to the Metropolitan. Manchester to Dover via Watkin lines was the main prize – and it might not have stopped at Dover, for Watkin was also very active in advocating a Channel tunnel and had dreams of connecting his native Manchester with Paris by rail all the way.

By now, however, Watkin was leaving more and more of the running of the company to John Bell, who became his successor on 5 May 1894 when Watkin retired, through illness, from the boards of the Metropolitan and his other lines. Bell did not get on with William Pollitt, general manager of the M.S. & L., and relations between the two companies became steadily worse. After a good deal of argument, in which an unfinished tower built at Wembley by Watkin to rival the Eiffel Tower figured prominently, the agreement on running powers was modified, and the M.S. & L. ran over the Metropolitan's tracks from Quainton Road to Canfield Place, near Finchley Road, only. Two extra tracks were built south of Harrow-on-the-Hill specially for M.S. & L. traffic, and that railway built its own London terminus at Marylebone. By an Act of 1897 the M.S. & L. became the Great Central Railway, the last of the main lines to reach London. Regular passenger trains began running from Marylebone on 15 March 1899; by agreement with the Metropolitan they were not allowed to stop at stations south of Harrow, so that the Metropolitan's suburban service was to some extent protected from the newcomer. There were no platforms at stations south of Harrow on the Great Central tracks, except for an emergency pair, during the 1939–45 war, at Neasden.

With this we have nearly completed the tale of steam lines in the 19th century, but there are a few points to be cleared up and lines to be mentioned.

The Whitechapel & Bow Railway was promoted and incorporated under an Act of 1897 to build a connecting line between the District's Whitechapel terminus and the London, Tilbury & Southend Railway's line at Bow. It was opened on 2 June 1902 and was jointly owned by the District and the L.T.S.R. It was worked by the District, some trains running over it to the L.T.S.R. station at East Ham and some right through to Upminster.

An Act of 1894 gave powers to a separate company, the Ealing & South Harrow Railway Company, to build a line between those two points. The company made an agreement with the District and started to build in 1898, finishing the line the next year. The line did not come into use, however, at this time. Another authorized line, the Harrow & Uxbridge Railway, was intended to make an end-on junction with the Ealing & South Harrow; this also had a working agreement with the District. The work was slow in starting, apparently because of lack of money, and the scheme came under the control of the Metropolitan. A new Act of 1899 reduced the scheme to a connecting line from South Harrow to Rayners Lane but left the Metropolitan to build the line from Harrow to Uxbridge, which was opened on 4 July 1904, with steam traction. The connecting line from Rayners Lane to South Harrow was built but not connected to the District tracks because the two companies could not agree about the powers granted in the Act for the District to run over the Uxbridge branch. South Harrow had its first services on 28 June 1903, by District electric trains, but the Rayners Lane–South Harrow line was used only for coal traffic (by the Metropolitan) until it was officially connected up and District electric trains began to run through to Uxbridge on 1 March 1910.

IV The East London Railway: the Birth of the Tunnelling Shield

AS IT HAS formed part of the steam story, it is as well to deal here with the East London Railway. This was part of the Watkin empire and was used by both Metropolitan and District trains, as we have seen, but it did not become the full responsibility of London Transport until nationalization in 1948.

The East London owed its existence to what was intended to be a pioneer road tunnel under the Thames. Thames tunnel schemes were put forward in 1798 and 1802, and work started on this second scheme, which was for a tunnel between Rotherhithe and Limehouse. The first shaft struck snags, and Robert Vazie, whose idea the tunnel was, called in Richard Trevithick, the amazing Cornish engineer who left his mark on locomotive development as well as many other things, to help him. The Thames Archway Company, which had been formed to exploit Vazie's plans, soon dismissed Vazie and gave Trevithick full charge. He decided that a team of Cornish miners should first drive a pilot tunnel 5 ft. high and 3 ft. wide. Starting from the Rotherhithe bank, he got to low water mark on the Limehouse side, with 1,000 ft. of tunnel out of 1,200 ft. built, before, on 26 January 1808, the river broke in and ruined the works. Although Trevithick put forward an idea which has since been used with great success – laying large pipes under the protection of cofferdams to make the tunnel – the company's consultants said the tunnel was impossible to build, and the whole idea was abandoned.

In 1818, however, Marc Brunel patented a shield for tunnelling. One of the Thames Archway promoters heard of it and talked to Brunel, and a new company, the Thames Tunnel Company, was formed to build the tunnel between Rotherhithe and Wapping, using the shield. An Act received Royal Assent in 1825, but the work was already in hand by then.

Marc Brunel's shield was the world's first, and it was a development of it which made all the London deep tube lines possible, so it is worth describing in some detail. It was built in Henry Maudslay's works at Lambeth and consisted of 12 massive frames, each 3 ft. wide and 21 ft. 4 in. high, in cast iron. Each frame was divided into three compartments, one above the other, making 36 compartments in all. Massive plates below the frames served to support them, and other plates held up the ground above. Similar plates were provided at the sides of the outer frames. The whole formed a rectangular box with an open front. This opening was closed by stout oak planks across each of the 36 compartments, the planks (or 'poling boards') being pressed against the face of the excavation by adjustable 'poling screws', one end of which fitted in a recess in the plank and the other in a recess in the frame. Each plank had two poling screws to support it, and the screws could be adjusted within a range of 4½ in.

One man worked in each compartment, the method being to remove one plank, cut away the ground behind to a depth of 4½ in., put the plank back with the poling screws extended, and then repeat the performance until all the ground beyond the compartment had been cut away for 4½ in. A staging on wheels behind the shield had a hoist for carrying away the spoil.

Bricklayers building the tunnel lining worked back-to-back with the men at the shield, and, when the earth had been cut away, jacks, using the newly-completed brickwork as an anchorage, thrust the whole shield forward 4½ in. As the frames could not be moved with the poling screws in place, arrangements were provided which allowed the poling screws of one frame to be supported on those on each side of it. The frame itself could then be moved forward, the retracted screws put back on their proper frame, and the process repeated for the neighbouring frames until all had been moved forward. The entire cycle then started again.

Except for the 4½ in. ring left when the shield was thrust forward, the tunnel was thus supported at all times by the shield or the brickwork.

The first resident engineer was William Armstrong, but he resigned because of ill-health the following April (1826), and his place was taken by the 20-year-old Isambard Kingdom Brunel, later to become famous for his work on the Great Western Railway. He was the son of Marc (afterwards Sir Marc) Brunel.

The tale of the struggles of the tunnel builders has been told elsewhere. The river broke in, the money ran out, the incomplete tunnel became a sideshow known derisively as the 'Great Bore'. Eventually work started again, and the break-through was made in

1841, the first person to pass through the narrow hole being the three-year-old son of I. K. Brunel. The boy's grandfather was knighted for that day's work. The opening ceremony was held on 25 March 1843, and an official procession, with band, marched through the western arch of the tunnel, which was divided internally although it had been cut as one tunnel, and back along the eastern arch. The procession had to climb up and down stairways at each end, for the approaches which would take vehicles down to and up from the tunnel had not yet been built. They never were built, for the money was not there, and the Thames Tunnel remained for many years a pedestrian subway and something of a white elephant.

In 1865 the tunnel was acquired by the East London Railway (which never ran a train of its own) and in 1869 the railway through the tunnel was opened from the south to a station at Wapping with a train service of 23 trains a day in each direction, the service being worked by the London, Brighton & South Coast Railway, with which there was a physical connection at New Cross. The East London opened a branch between Surrey Docks and Old Kent Road in 1871, and in 1876 the line was extended from Wapping to Bishopsgate Junction on the Great Eastern Railway, enabling the L.B. & S.C. service to be extended to Liverpool Street. The East London was also connected to the South Eastern Railway and the L.B. & S.C.R. Up line in this year. Some trains were projected southwards to Croydon. In 1877 through trains began to run via the East London to Brighton; these continued for six years, though in the later stages the service was reduced to through coaches only.

Three years later, in 1880, the South Eastern Railway started running from Addiscombe Road to Liverpool Street via New Cross (S.E.R.). The service was later diverted to terminate at St. Mary's. Trains to St. Mary's ran over the Metropolitan and District joint Whitechapel curve, 22 ch. in length, from the East London Railway. This curve was opened on 3 March 1884, and St. Mary's station was opened on the same day. The station was renamed St. Mary's (Whitechapel Road) on 26 January 1923, and was abandoned on 30 April 1938. The Whitechapel curve was closed from 3 December 1906 to 31 March 1913, and was again closed to public traffic on 6 October 1941.

The Metropolitan and District railways began providing services under a new working agreement on 6 October 1884, and the S.E.R. trains were withdrawn. Also represented on the joint committee established were the L.B. & S.C.R., the S.E.R., the London, Chatham & Dover Railway, and the Great Eastern, which worked all freight services through the tunnel and, from 1886, the passenger trains which terminated at Liverpool Street.

The District services ceased on 31 July 1905, because of the electrification of the District Line, but the L.B. & S.C.R. increased its existing service between Peckham Rye, New Cross, and Shoreditch. For the same reason, the Metropolitan services were replaced in December 1906 by a limited S.E.R. service between New Cross and Whitechapel. The Shoreditch–Peckham Rye service was withdrawn in 1911, as were through trains south of New Cross.

In 1913 the East London line was electrified, without interference to traffic, and the passenger service was taken over by the Metropolitan from 31 March. Electric trains passed through the tunnel for the first time, running from New Cross to South Kensington via Baker Street, and also between Shoreditch and the two New Cross stations. (The L.B. & S.C.R. station at New Cross was renamed 'New Cross Gate' on 1 August 1923.) The western terminus was changed in February 1914 to Hammersmith (Hammersmith & City). The Metropolitan Railway took over the management of the line from 1 July 1921, and in 1925 the East London was acquired, under the Southern Railway Act, 1925, by the newly-formed Southern Railway, but was leased to the joint committee, then consisting of the S.R., L.N.E.R., Metropolitan, and District. The London Passenger Transport Board became responsible for passenger service operation in 1933; in 1941 the service to Hammersmith ceased and trains terminated at Whitechapel (Shoreditch in peak hours).

When the railways were nationalized in 1948, the line passed to the London Transport Executive. It is a tribute to the sound design of Marc Brunel and to the good workmanship insisted on by I. K. Brunel that the tunnel has withstood for so long the vibration (entirely unforeseen by the builders) of frequent steam and electric train services.

The present southern ends of the East London Line are 889 ft. from the buffer stops at New Cross station on one section of the line and 1,525 ft. from Canal Junction on the other section of line, which runs to New Cross Gate station, the Southern Region of British Railways being responsible for the remaining track into both stations.

A hoist installed in 1900 was used at one time to transfer freight vehicles – for attachment to passenger trains on the East London –

from the former Great Eastern Railway Spitalfields depot to sidings on the East London immediately beneath the depot. These sidings were on the east side of the line between Whitechapel and Shoreditch. The hoist has not been in use for some years.

The engineer to the East London Railway was Sir John Hawkshaw (1811–1891), who had a number of connections with I. K. Brunel. In 1838, for example, he reported, at the request of the Great Western Railway, on the advisability of continuing the use of Brunel's broad gauge – and came down against the broad gauge.

Access to the platforms at Wapping station is by one of the circular shafts of the original Thames Tunnel and the pillar facing the entrance of the station carries a slate plaque in memory of Sir Marc Brunel. It bears the words:

> '*The tunnel which runs under the Thames from this station was the first tunnel for public traffic ever to be driven beneath a river.*
>
> '*It was designed by Sir Marc Isambard Brunel* (1769–1849) *and completed in* 1843. *His son Isambard Kingdom Brunel* (1806–1859) *was engineer-in-charge from* 1825 to 1828.
>
> '*Erected by London Transport in* 1959.'

V Metropolitan and District Rolling Stock

STEAM LOCOMOTIVES worked passenger trains on the Metropolitan right down to 9 September 1961, but as our main story will shortly switch to electrically-operated railways, this seems as good a place as any to review the steam fleet of the Underground. The earliest Fowler/Beyer, Peacock locomotives have already been dealt with, and, as we have said, they were used for both Metropolitan and District train working. With the extension of the Metropolitan Railway into Middlesex, Hertfordshire, and Buckinghamshire during the 1880s and early '90s, however, came the need for additional locomotives. Three more small classes, all tank engines, were added to the stud. Four 0–4–4 'C' class locomotives were built by Neilson's in 1891, very much to South Eastern Railway design. These were followed, in 1894/5, by six Sharp, Stewart 2–4–0 tanks, known as the 'D' class, which much resembled Barry Railway designs. Then, in 1896, the Metropolitan put into service the first of the 'E' class 0–4–4s, designed by its own locomotive superintendent, Mr. T. F. Clark; the first three were built in the Metropolitan works at Neasden, and one of them was given the number '1', replacing the original 'A' class locomotive of that number. Four more 'E' class tanks were built by Hawthorn, Leslie in 1900–01, and in the latter year the 'F' class also appeared. This class consisted of four 0–6–2 tanks built by the Yorkshire Engine Company specifically for freight working. Meanwhile, in 1897 and 1899, two Peckett 0–6–0 saddle tanks were put into service for yard work at Finchley Road and Harrow.

The next steam locomotives to be delivered to the Metropolitan were the four 0–6–4 'G' class tanks of Yorkshire Engine Company manufacture, which were put into service late in 1915. Being much larger than any earlier Metropolitan locomotives, they were the pride of the railway and were given names. The first three, Nos. 94–96, were named *Lord Aberconway*, *Robert H. Selbie*, and *Charles Jones*, after the company's chairman, general manager, and chief electrical and locomotive engineer respectively. The fourth, No.

97, bore the name *Brill.* Brill was at that time the most distant point of the Metropolitan territory from Baker Street, some 51 miles away.

In 1920–21 appeared the 'H' class, eight in number and built by Kerr, Stuart & Co. to the design of Mr. Charles Jones. These 4–4–4 tank locomotives had a particularly handsome, well-balanced appearance. They were followed by the still larger and more powerful 2–6–4 tanks of the 'K' class, the largest locomotives owned by the Metropolitan. With their 24,400 lb. tractive effort, these six locomotives were ideal for hauling the heavier freight trains on the outer parts of the system. They were built by Armstrong, Whitworth using parts made at Woolwich Arsenal after the 1914–18 War. The parts were of South Eastern & Chatham Railway design and were originally intended for 2–6–0 tender locomotives.

There were some other locomotives outside these classes. The five 0–6–0 tanks built by the Worcester Engine Company in 1868 for the originally separate St. John's Wood Railway proved wastefully powerful, so their London career was short-lived and they left the Metropolitan after a few years for service on other railways. There were also the Aveling & Porter geared locomotives from the Brill branch and the little Manning Wardle 0–6–0 tank *Nellie*, used by the contractors for the Uxbridge line, which subsequently passed to the Metropolitan for use as a shunting locomotive at Neasden. Two similar Manning Wardle saddle tanks, *Brill* and *Wotton No.2*, worked on the Brill line and were taken over when the line passed to the Metropolitan. A third 0–6–0 tank, originally named *Huddersfield*, but renamed *Wotton*, had been scrapped in pre-Metropolitan days.

When London Transport assumed control of the Metropolitan in 1933, there were still over 30 steam locomotives on the line, including the complete 'E', 'F', 'G', 'H', and 'K' classes and the two Peckett saddle tanks. There were also representatives of the 'A' class. The progressive electrification of the Metropolitan, from 1905 onwards, brought about a corresponding decrease in the need for steam locomotives. From 1925 only the lines north of Rickmansworth required steam motive power for passenger duties. The Metropolitan, however, unlike the other London Underground lines, had a considerable volume of freight traffic, and steam engines were still required to deal with it.

Among the schemes incorporated in London Transport's 1935–40 New Works Programme was a comprehensive plan to improve the Metropolitan Line, including the provision of a large new depot on the former locomotive works and carriage shed site at Neasden. As steam motive power was to be eliminated from the Metropolitan under this programme and space was needed for the work at Neasden depot, responsibility for the provision of steam locomotives for passenger trains north of Rickmansworth and for freight working was transferred to the London & North Eastern Railway on 1 November 1937. The 18 locomotives of the Metropolitan's 'G', 'H', and 'K' classes were handed over to the L.N.E.R. on the same date, and for a time they continued to perform their usual work. London Transport retained thirteen steam locomotives, some having been scrapped between 1933 and 1937, for miscellaneous engineer's duties. These were replaced in postwar years by ex-Western Region 0–6–0 pannier tank locomotives, which have themselves now given way to electric and diesel locomotives. The last steam locomotive was withdrawn on Sunday, 6 June 1971.

The District Railway had only one main type of engine, which differed only in minor details from those of the same type for the Metropolitan. The later locomotives of the series were improved in some respects, e.g., a higher boiler pressure, and the earlier ones were modified to the same standard when they passed through the shops.

In 1931 two 0–6–0 outside cylinder side tank locomotives were built to work on the District (but not for passenger duties). They were by Hunslet of Leeds and were withdrawn in 1963.

The earliest Metropolitan coaching stock consisted of 'rigid' eight-wheelers with the wheels in groups of four at each end so that they resembled, at first glance, bogie vehicles. One of these coaches ran up to the last on the Brill branch; in 196 fourteen of them were seen near Bordeaux in France, apparently in good order (though somewhat modified by the addition of a corridor) in the service of the Reseau des Landes de la Gironde et Ligne Lacanau a l'Ocean.

In 1870 (the prototype appeared the year before) 24 'twin-carriages' – short vehicles close-coupled – appeared.

With the delivery of the 'Ashbury' stock, the Metropolitan's first bogie stock, in the late 1890s, the longer-distance trains were usually made up with these coaches, and they remained in use on the Aylesbury trains until converted for electric multiple-unit operation between 1906 and 1924. Six of these vehicles were re-converted for steam haulage and used on the Chesham branch until withdrawn in September 1960. Four are still in the hands of the 'Bluebell Railway'.

There followed the 'Dreadnoughts', which gradually superseded the 'Ashbury' stock on 'main-line' trains. There were 92 of these coaches, some two-thirds of which lasted to the end of steam days. The 54-ft. 'Dreadnoughts' were like suburban coaches on most of the main lines into London. The compartment layout – for many years the compartments in some vehicles were connected in threes by a central gangway – with swing doors, side buffers, screw-link couplings, and vacuum brakes showed features usually associated with a main line rather than an underground railway. However, the provision of current collector shoes on the outer bogie of the brake vehicle was unusual. These shoes enabled current, through a bus line, to reach the comparatively short wheel-base locomotive when its own shoes were out of contact with the conductor rails at crossings. The shoes also collected current for train heating in the electrified area. Steam heating by the usual method was employed when steam haulage was in use.

Two other vehicles which spent most of their lives coupled with 'Dreadnoughts' must be mentioned. These were the two Pullman cars, *Mayflower* and *Galatea*, which were put into service on 1 June 1910 in 'main-line' trains between the City or Baker Street and Aylesbury or Chesham making several journeys a day, including late evening trips. At one time they also operated as far out as Verney Junction. At first, they worked with 'Ashbury' stock, but later they were transferred to 'Dreadnought' trains. The two cars were provided by and remained the property of the Pullman Car Company, which raised a supplementary fee of 6*d*. for a journey anywhere between London and Rickmansworth or 1*s*. for a journey to, or between, any stations north of Rickmansworth. The cars themselves were maintained by the Metropolitan, but internal fittings, such as carpets and furnishings, were the maintenance responsibility of the Pullman company. The 1939–45 war brought about their withdrawal, and they last operated on 7 October 1939.

In 1927, fifteen vehicles were converted for use in electric multiple-unit trains, five coaches being marshalled between new driving motor coaches to make three of the first trains of what was later known as the 'T' stock. Ten further coaches were similarly converted at various dates by London Transport. The 'T' stock, which was always electric stock, will be described later. All this stock has now been withdrawn.

The District line was originally worked by the Metropolitan with Metropolitan locomotives and coaches, but the District needed its own when it made its bid for independence. It bought four-wheel stock measuring under 30 ft. over the buffers. The initial order was for 152 coaches, half of which were third class and the rest first and second class in equal numbers. The first-class compartments seated 10, five on each side, and there were four compartments to each vehicle. Second- and third-class compartments were similar, but narrower, so that five were squeezed into the space occupied by four in the first class. According to accounts of the time, the first class was in fact very comfortable, but the second and third probably left much to be desired by modern standards. The coaches were provided with gas lighting, the gas being carried in bags in the roof, replenished as required at Kensington High Street (which was the coaling and watering point for District locomotives) and at Mansion House. Oil gas was substituted later and was safer, as it was carried compressed in cylinders. Both the Metropolitan and District were exempted from the requirement of the Railway Regulation Act of 1868 that a smoking carriage had to be attached to any train which was made up with more than one carriage for each class of traveller. The Act provided for railways to be excused in special circumstances, and the fact that the District and Metropolitan were underground lines was evidently special circumstance enough. In fact, however, both railways introduced such carriages in the autumn of 1874 in deference to popular demand.

No other type of coach was purchased by the District for steam services, but it bought more of the original type from time to time. At the end of steam operation it had 215 third-class coaches, 92 second, and 87 first, as well as one composite coach.

VI The First Tube Railways: City & South London

WE NOW COME to a different sort of underground railway. Those we have considered so far were all built near the surface. Where they could, they used the cut-and-cover method of construction. Where they had to tunnel they used the traditional railway tunnelling methods – except Sir Marc Brunel with his Thames Tunnel – and it is here that we take up the story again.

When the iron cylinders for the Lambeth suspension bridge were being sunk in 1862, the resident engineer, Peter William Barlow (a former railway engineer) had the idea that similar tubes of iron might be built horizontally to form tunnels. Working on the earlier Brunel shield idea, Barlow devised a new form of circular shield which he patented in 1864. He also thought of a transport system which could use his new tunnels, and in 1867 he published a pamphlet setting out an idea for a network of tunnels in which small cars would run – the tunnels would be only 8 ft. in diameter – each holding 12 passengers. The cars would be pushed by hand where gravity would not supply the force. He intended to have all the stations at a constant depth below ground and suggested that the tunnels should be built in sections at different levels to make this possible. The cars would be raised or lowered from one level to another by lifts.

This idea was too good to waste, and in 1868 a company, the Tower Subway Company, was formed to build a tube tunnel beneath the Thames. The company started operations early in 1869, and it built, with Barlow as engineer and a pupil of his, James Henry Greathead, as contractor, a tunnel 1,340 ft. long which ran from Great Tower Hill to Vine Street, Southwark. The single tunnel was lined with cast-iron segments giving a clear internal diameter of 6 ft. 7¾ in. It was reached at each end by shafts 10 ft. in diameter and more than 50 ft. deep. The ironwork was slightly smaller than the bore made with the shield, and the space between the iron and the earth was filled with liquid cement – a principle which has been retained for this type of work ever since. The shield itself was a cylinder which was pushed forward by screw jacks as miners inside it cut the earth away. As the shield moved forward, the segments were erected at once to support the new tunnel, and the shield was pushed forward again, the jacks now pushing against the newly-installed segments. The tunnel sloped downwards to a point under the centre of the river and then rose again as it approached the other bank. At its greatest depth it was 66 ft. below high water level.

Once the tunnel had been completed the machinery was installed. The shafts received steam-driven lifts and a 2 ft. 6 in. gauge railway track was laid along the tunnel itself. On this track was placed a car 10 ft. long with seats for 12 or 14 at a pinch, if accounts of the day are to be believed. Barlow now had the track and car he had envisaged, but he stopped short at using manpower to move the car and installed cable haulage operated by two 4 h.p. steam engines. The formal opening took place on 2 August 1870, although the line had been working on an experimental basis for some months before that.

Here then, at last, was the first tube railway in the world. It offered two classes of ticket, though not of travel, the more expensive (2*d.* as against 1*d.*) ticket merely giving priority in the lift cages. Unfortunately, the ingenuity of this first tube was greater than its capacity. Not enough people could be carried in the small car to pay for the cost of the equipment and its working. There were also mechanical troubles, and after a few months the cable car ceased to operate. The car was removed, the track lifted, and lifts dismantled. Then a spiral wooden staircase was put in each shaft and a footway along the tunnel, and the first tube railway became a toll subway for pedestrians who paid a halfpenny each to use it. In this guise the tube played a useful part in the lives of Londoners until Tower Bridge opened in 1894 and Londoners could walk over the river instead. Even then its life was not finished. It was used to carry the pipes of the London Hydraulic Power Company. It is still there today, and it still carries the hydraulic mains as well as two mains belonging to the Metropolitan Water Board.

There might have been other such subways, for Barlow had powers to build one between the City and Southwark and later actually began work on one between North and South Woolwich. The failure of the Tower Subway, however, caused both these schemes to be abandoned.

Barlow had sown the seeds and also had fired the imagination of Greathead, whose name has become attached to the shield which

Brunel and then Barlow had laboured to perfect. Greathead was soon to use it to build the first major underground railway in deep tube tunnels.

The first deep-level railway, with electric traction, to be authorized was the Charing Cross & Waterloo Electric Railway, which obtained its Act in 1882. This line was to run from Trafalgar Square to Waterloo station and to have twin tubes under the Thames, though there would have been double-track tunnels clear of the river. The civil engineering work was to be carried out under Henry Law and George Chatterton; the electrical engineer was Dr. C. W. Siemens. This was progress, indeed, for it was only in 1879 that Dr. Werner von Siemens had demonstrated the first electric railway in the world at a Berlin exhibition.

Another proposal, for a London Central Railway Company line from the northern end of the Charing Cross & Waterloo line to St. Martins-le-Grand, via Oxford Street, came before Parliament in 1884 but was turned down on the grounds that Parliament wished first to see whether the earlier part of the line was successful. This setback affected the earlier company, which saw chances of swift expansion to be unlikely, and work on its scheme was abandoned in 1885 after about 60 ft. of tunnel had been built under Northumberland Avenue.

When Greathead came on the scene in 1884 it was not as an advocate of electric traction. He had been impressed with the cable tramway introduced by Andrew Hallidie in San Francisco, on the Clay Street Hill Railroad, in 1873, and with other lines built afterwards on the same system, including the Highgate Hill tramway in London in this same year of 1884. He now joined in applying for an Act to build a twin-tunnel tube railway from near the northern end of London Bridge to the Elephant & Castle. It was largely Greathead's performance when giving evidence in committee which made sure the Act was passed, despite great opposition.

The City of London & Southwark Subway Company, as the promoters of the new scheme became, was incorporated on 28 July 1884. Greathead was the engineer with Sir Benjamin Baker and Sir John Fowler as consultants. The prospectus of the company promised 12 per cent dividends.

The terminus at the City end was at the junction of King William Street and Arthur Street (now Monument Street); the station building itself was No. 46 King William Street. In those days the tubes, like the sub-surface lines, found it expedient to avoid legal arguments and compensation by following the line of the streets above. This meant that the City terminus had to be built to run roughly east and west and that the line had to curve round just after leaving the station to pass under the river. It ran under Arthur Street, which was so narrow that the two tunnels had to run one above the other to keep beneath the street itself, and then under Swan Lane, at the end of which, in those days, stood Old Swan Pier. South of the river, the line was to pass under Borough High Street and Newington Causeway to the Elephant, a total distance of 1½ miles. Intermediate stations were to be built at Denman Street and Great Dover Street (Borough).

In February 1886 the main contract for the tunnels and stations was placed with Edmund Gabbutt, a Liverpool contractor. Preparations began in May, and work started in October from a shaft sunk from a temporary staging behind the Old Swan Pier. From this shaft the driving of the upper (up line) tunnel southwards began the same month. The lower (down) tunnel was not started until the following March, and then it was driven so that it rose to the same level as the up tunnel, and to the west of it, on the south side of the river. These tunnels were 10 ft. 2 in. in diameter and accommodated a standard-gauge railway track.

In the following year powers were obtained to continue the line southwards to Stockwell, making the line just over three miles in length. It was decided that the tunnels on this section should be 10 ft. 6 in. in diameter because the gradients were easier and the trains could be run at a higher speed. The engine house to be built at the Elephant would drive one cable for the City section at 10 m.p.h. and another for the Stockwell section at 12 m.p.h. The contract for the new section of the line was let to Walter Scott & Co., of Newcastle, the same firm also completing the City section when ill-health caused Edmund Gabbutt to withdraw.

Contracts for the lifts had been placed, and so had those for the cable apparatus, but doubts began to be expressed about the wisdom of cable working. Electric traction had already been mooted for other lines, as we have seen, and what really seems to have turned the scales was the success of the electrically-operated Bessbook & Newry Railway in Ireland, opened in 1885. That electric traction was practicable had already been shown in Great Britain, for Magnus Volk had opened his electric railway at Brighton in 1883.

The technical press was already drawing the attention of the chairman of the City of London & Southwark, Charles Grey Mott, to the advantages of electric traction, and he sought professional advice. In its report for the half-year in August 1888, the board told the shareholders that experiments were to be made with electric traction pending a decision on its use. One of the most famous signal engineers of the day, C. E. Spagnoletti, who has already been mentioned in connection with the signalling of the Metropolitan Railway, was called in as consultant on electric traction. This caused some comment at the time, as he had had no experience in this field, but there is no reason to doubt that his advice was sound. Engineers were still all-rounders in those days.

In 1889 a contract was placed with Mather & Platt Ltd., who undertook to supply the power necessary to run a three-minute service from each station and to run the trains at a higher average speed than those of the Inner Circle. They also gave a guaranteed cost per train-mile for a period of two years – lower than the cost of steam working if steam working had been allowed. An experimental train was to be provided by the contractors, and it was expected that this would be ready in April 1889.

Meanwhile, work went on on the stations and tunnels. The King William Street terminus site was reached by a shaft from above, but eventually most of the debris from the station works and the City end of the tunnels went out by the shaft in the river at Old Swan Pier. When the work was completed, this shaft was sealed and made watertight over the tunnels and the staging was removed. At platform level the station had a single track with a platform on each side – a design suitable for cable operation but not electric. The street was reached by two hydraulic lifts running in a single 25 ft. diameter shaft. The gas-lit station was modified in 1895 (under traffic!) and became a two-track layout with an island platform between the two tracks. At the Stockwell end a 1-in-3½ incline led from the station to the rolling stock depot at the side of Spurgeon's Orphanage in the Clapham Road. Cable haulage was needed to take stock up this incline. The intermediate stations were Borough, Elephant & Castle, Kennington, and Oval.

The station tunnels had a 3 ft. deep brick lining, and the terminal stations had tunnels 26 ft. wide and 20 ft. high. At intermediate stations there were tunnels for each line, each tunnel being 20 ft. wide, 16 ft. high, and 200 ft. long. From the first, the Stockwell terminus had an island platform with a track on each side. King William Street and Stockwell both had hydraulic buffers.

Experimental running began in December 1889 with one locomotive and two coaches. The track was not yet complete, nor was the generating station at Stockwell, so current was taken, on the three-rail system, from a temporary generating station at the Borough, from which point the rails to the City were complete. The first tunnel went through to Stockwell in January 1890, and a second, geared, locomotive arrived for trials in February. On 7 March the company felt sufficiently confident of progress to take the Lord Mayor and other guests from the City to the Elephant. They also proposed to take them back again to a special luncheon, but the water company, having found some defect, turned off the supply of water to the temporary generating plant, which had to be hastily shut down. The party did get back by rail, an hour late, but the effect on the food – and tempers – is not known. Everyone had recovered enough to take the Metropolitan Railway directors on a similar trip the following week.

The formal opening was on 4 November 1890; it was performed by the Prince of Wales (afterwards King Edward VII). In the meantime, the company's name had been changed to the City & South London Railway to match its enlarged status – still further enlarged by the granting of Parliamentary authority to continue the line to Clapham – and it was under this name that the line was opened. The party travelled from King William Street to Oval to look at the works and equipment, and then on to Stockwell for lunch in a marquee in the rolling-stock depot. The general manager had been appointed – T. C. Jenkin, a former London, Tilbury & Southend Railway accountant – and so had the resident engineer, who was Basil (later Sir Basil) Mott. Pleased as they no doubt were with the ceremony and the electric locomotive specially painted for the occasion in cream and grey and named *Princess of Wales*, they were probably even more pleased to receive on the same day permission from the Board of Trade to open the line for public traffic. The first electric tube railway was in business at last. Even now, however, there was a delay while the staff familiarized themselves with their work and empty trains ran up and down the line, but public service started eventually on Thursday, 18 December 1890.

The line started working with 14 locomotives built by Mather & Platt at their Salford Iron Works to the design of Dr. Edward Hopkinson. They had doors at the ends, measured 14 ft. over the centre buffers, weighed about 10 tons, and were carried on four 27-in. wheels. Each of the axles was driven by a 50-h.p. motor with its armature built directly on the axles, the first time this arrangement, obviating gearing, had been used. The second trial locomotive, which *was* geared, was so noisy that it was tucked away and used only in emergency. (It was said to be audible at one station when starting from the next down the line.) The two motors were connected permanently in series and took power at 500V. d.c. through cast-iron flat collector shoes from the third rail. This was a channel-section steel rail carried on glass insulators and mounted between the rails about a foot from the left-hand rail (as one left the City).

The locomotives had air brakes but no air pumps, relying on large reservoirs which were recharged at Stockwell on each trip. There was no 'dead man's handle' in those days to ensure that power was cut off and brakes were applied if anything happened to the driver, so an assistant had to be carried on the locomotive. Originally these locomotives were a dark red, or red-brown, but they soon blossomed forth in orange chrome in three panels on each side, with black and yellow borders to the panels.

These little locomotives, one of which can still be seen in the Science Museum at South Kensington, pulled three-car trains. The cars – 30 of them – were built by the Ashbury Railway Carriage & Iron Co. Each car had seats for 32, arranged in two long seats facing each other across the car, and the bogie frames were extended beyond the wooden body to provide platforms for the guards or attendants, and incidentally to give a semi-circular end to the frame in lieu of headstocks. As there were no buffers on the cars, this arrangement also served as a bumper if required. The attendants rode between the ends of the cars on their platforms and opened and closed lattice gates, letting people into or out of the cars through doors in the ends of the wooden bodies via the platforms and the lattice gates. The attendants also told passengers where they were, for the upholstery was carried up nearly to the roof, leaving only slit windows for ventilation. This was done, apparently, on the assumption that there was no need for windows because there was nothing to see. These cars quickly earned the name of 'padded cells' – perhaps the company thought passengers needed them, because it also thought it necessary to forbid passengers to ride on the roof of the train! One car of each train was set aside for smokers, and it is said that ladies were forbidden to enter it. Each car had four electric lamps, but they were only of 16 candlepower each and not very efficient. They were always short of current, a situation which also made it necessary for the stations to be provided with gas instead of electric lamps. There is a 'padded cell' car in the London Transport Museum.

At first there was a train every five minutes and the speed worked out at about 11½ m.p.h. including stops. The hydraulic lifts at the stations, power for which was produced at Stockwell and carried through the tunnels in a main at 1,240 lb. per sq. in., took away the disadvantages of a deep line, and the railway prospered. Its two-penny fare seems to have been well calculated, and in its first two weeks it carried 165,000 passengers. It was safe, using a version of Spagnoletti's lock-and-block signalling apparatus with mechanically-operated signals, and, of course, it was clean and quick. It did not run on Sundays until 5 April 1891.

The first extension to the railway after the opening date was to Moorgate, forming part of an extension to the Angel which had been authorized in 1893. The Act concerned also gave powers to replace King William Street, which was so awkwardly placed that the down line had to negotiate a 1 in 14 gradient on leaving it, by a station at the Bank. It also provided for a station near the south side of London Bridge. The avoiding line needed to connect these two stations left the original line north of Borough station and passed under the Thames east of London Bridge, leaving the original tunnels under the river and the original terminus deserted. The line to Moorgate was opened on 25 February 1900. The deserted tunnels were blocked off from the rest of the line during the last war to avoid any risk of flooding, and parts of the tunnels were used as air raid shelters. Parts are still used for storage, but the under-river sections remain empty.

The extension used an improved signalling system which had also been applied to the 'main line'. Electric lamps had replaced oil and gas in the signals, and the original long block sections, which extended from the starting signal at one station to the starting signal at the next (or the buffer stops at the termini), were shortened by adding an outer home signal to the home signal which protected a train at a platform – really only an emergency signal. To make sure that a section was clear, an ingenious form of 'last axle' indicator was used. This consisted of an insulated plate mounted on each side of the tunnel and a special brush on the last car of each train. When the brush touched the plate it completed a block release circuit through the rails. This was the first apparatus of this type on an underground railway. The effect was that as soon as a train was known to have come within the protection of the outer home signal that signal could be put at danger and the starting signal at the station in rear could be lowered to allow another train to follow. There were no distant signals on the line. Repeaters were provided for the signals where necessary, and there were some minor changes, but broadly this form of signalling lasted until replaced after the 1914–18 war by automatic signalling.

The extension tunnels were 11 ft. 6 in. in diameter, this size being adopted in an effort to improve ventilation, but it seems not to have had the desired effect, as it was only carried out to Moorgate. London Bridge and Bank stations were built with two platforms on the same level and connecting passages, now a common plan. Incidentally, £540 per sq. yd. was paid for the Bank station site even in those days. The intermediate stations on the original line had platforms at different levels, staggered so that one overlapped the other by many yards; generally they seemed to have nothing but the station name and ticket office in common. At London Bridge and Bank, however, one eccentricity – caused by geography – remained in that the trains kept to the right-hand track instead of the left. This was corrected between the Bank and Moorgate, where one line passed over the other to restore normal left-hand running.

An extension was opened to the Angel on 17 November 1901. Meanwhile, the southern extension to Clapham Common, authorized in the 1890 Act, was opened on 3 June 1900. Powers to extend from the Angel to Euston were obtained in 1903 and the line was opened officially to this station on 11 May 1907, public traffic beginning the next day. The Angel extension had two intermediate stations, Old Street and City Road (the latter closed in 1922); there was one station, King's Cross, between the Angel and Euston.

The new stations had electric lifts; at Euston, the Angel, and Clapham Common there was a single island platform in a 30 ft diameter tube. Electric lights were placed all along the tunnels at about this time so that a signalman could turn them on if a train was an unusually long time in any section and might be in trouble. As about the same time, two bare wires were affixed to the tunnel walls so that a train driver could lean out of his stopped train and fix a telephone handset to the wires anywhere in the tunnel. He could then speak to the signalman ahead and tell him what was wrong. These last two features have been incorporated in all the London Transport tunnels.

More locomotives and rolling stock were needed for all these extensions, and by 1907 there were 52 locomotives and 165 cars by various builders. The locomotives retained much the same appearance as the original 14 but were smoother in outline. They also had better control arrangements, air pumps for the air brake system, and electric headlamps. In an attempt to work four-car trains into King William Street, a four-car motor coach train, with the motors incorporated in the cars instead of in a separate locomotive, was tried in 1894. Not much is known about this train, which seems to have been a 'do-it-yourself' effort at Stockwell depot. The main reason for failure seems not to have been mechanical or electrical, but the time taken by the driver and his assistant to change ends at the terminus. By the time they had pushed their way through the crowds the train was already late in leaving.

The coaching stock seems to have improved slowly, the main step forward coming with the building and delivery by the Brush Company in 1907 of 30 all-steel cars of a greatly improved type.

Other improvements were a hydraulic car lift to obviate the use of the cable slope at Stockwell and the introduction in 1906 of five-car trains. In 1913, the C. & S.L.R. became part of the Underground Group, and a new chapter opened in its eventful life. Before we look at that, however, we must go back and see what other tubes were being built.

VII The Waterloo & City and the Central London

THE NEXT TUBE railway to appear on the scene was one which is not, and never has been, part of the London Transport system. It was built as an extension to the London & South Western Railway, which had always wanted to push into the City but had somehow missed its chance. It considered a full-scale deep-level line to take its trains into the City and also an elevated line, but both these solutions were turned down as immensely costly, and a deep-level electrically-operated tube railway seemed the only practicable answer if L.S.W.R. patrons were to be taken where most of them wanted to go – the City. An Act for a deep line, with twin tunnels, starting under Waterloo station and ending at a point near Mansion House was obtained in July 1893. The Act was obtained by the Waterloo & City Railway Company, but this was a matter of name only, the L.S.W.R. being the force behind it. Greathead was the engineer in partnership with the L.S.W.R. consulting engineer, W. R. Galbraith. The resident engineer was H. H. Dalrymple Hay.

Work on the line began in mid-1894. It ran under Stamford Street and then diagonally under the Thames to the north bank, reached near Blackfriars Bridge. From there it was a straight run up Queen Victoria Street to the Mansion House terminus (which was called City when the line was opened and renamed 'Bank' on 28 October 1940). The under-river section was excavated from cylinders sunk right through the river bed down to working level. Spoil was loaded direct into river barges from the top of the cylinders.

The Act allowed either electric or cable working, but the success of the City & South London ensured that electric working was adopted. The tunnels were much larger than those of the C.S.L.R., being a minimum of 12 ft. 1½ in. in diameter and allowing larger stock. The gauge was the standard 4 ft. 8½ in.

The Waterloo & City decided from the first not to use locomotives; four-car trains made up of motor cars and trailers were decided on. The cars were built in America, assembled at the L.S.W.R. Eastleigh

Works, and brought up to Waterloo by steam power. Trains drew power from a third (centre) rail, current being supplied from a small power station next to the line's low-level shops at Waterloo. One unusual feature was that power cables ran through the cars. (The modern multiple-unit principle is that low-voltage control lines only are carried through a train.)

The work was completed in 1897, and on 11 July 1898, the $1\frac{1}{2}$-mile line was opened by the Duke of Cambridge. It opened for public traffic on 8 August.

There are no intermediate stations on the line, and it has no physical connection with any other underground line. When stock needs overhaul, it is raised by the hoist at Waterloo to the main lines. The railway was taken over by the London & South Western Railway in 1907 and has come down into the hands of the Southern Region of British Railways. The original stock survived until 1940, when it was completely replaced by modern cars with power-operated doors.

The Waterloo & City is connected by passenger subways to the Northern and Bakerloo lines at Waterloo and by a long moving platform like a flattened-out escalator, known as a Trav-o-lator, to a common circulating area with the Northern and Central lines at the Bank. The Waterloo & City has its own tickets, issued by the Southern Region, and its own barrier staff.

The next tube line on the scene was destined to make a much greater mark than either of the earlier ones. The Central London Railway thrust itself impudently right across London to reach the City from the west, and Londoners took it to their hearts at once. Like the other lines, however, it was a long time being born.

The original Central London Railway Bill was drawn up to include three railways, the first from a point in the Bayswater Road to a point in Oxford Street just west of the junction of Old Quebec Street; the second from the end of railway No. 1 to a point in King William Street and the third from the end of No. 2 to junctions with the City of London & Southwark Subway at Arthur Street West. The scheme for this last junction was later abandoned. The Bill passed through the Commons in April–May 1890 but was rejected in July by the Lords.

Among the objectors was the Metropolitan Railway, which claimed that the proposed line was badly engineered and that the electric motive power would have to be replaced eventually by steam ('the only efficient form of railway motive power'). The District also objected, for the new line gave a short cut across the Inner Circle. Other objectors included the City Corporation, the Dean and Chapter of St. Paul's, and landowners and frontagers along the route.

Undismayed, the promoters made some concessions to the objectors and returned to Parliament in the next session with a new Bill which combined their original scheme and one originated by the London Central Subway, giving a railway running from Shepherd's Bush to Cornhill. The Bill passed through all its stages and received the Royal Assent on 5 August 1891. In 1892 a scheme for extending the line from the Bank to Liverpool Street, with a station at the Royal Exchange instead of that originally proposed to be in Cornhill, was approved by Parliament.

As soon as the 1891 Act was passed, the Central London Railway Company was able to prepare for the start of work. Greathead was an obvious choice as one of the engineers; so were Sir John Fowler and Sir Benjamin Baker as the others. The original chairman was Henry Tennant, formerly general manager of the North Eastern Railway, but in 1898 he retired from the chairmanship – he was by now an old man – in favour of Sir Henry Oakley, former general manager of the Great Northern Railway. J. H. Greathead died soon after work started, and his place was taken by Basil Mott, whom we first met in connection with the C.S.L.R.

After some delay, contracts for the tunnelling and structural work were let in the spring of 1896. There were three contractors: J. Price (Shepherd's Bush–Marble Arch), Walter Scott & Company (Marble Arch–Post Office), and G. Talbot (Post Office–Bank). Most of the tunnel was built through London clay, but hard rock, sand, and hard clay were encountered in one area.

The original stations were: Shepherd's Bush, Holland Park, Notting Hill Gate, Queen's Road (now Queensway), Lancaster Gate (built as Westbourne), Marble Arch, Bond Street (originally proposed as Davies Street), Oxford Circus, Tottenham Court Road, British Museum (closed in 1933 and replaced by new platforms at the reconstructed Piccadilly Line Holborn (Kingsway) station), Chancery Lane, Post Office (now St. Paul's), and Bank. The depot was at Shepherd's Bush, beyond the station.

A feature of the line at every station where it could be incorporated was a rising gradient of 1 in 60 at the approach to station platforms to help braking, and a fall of 1 in 30 for 100 yd. from each platform to help the train to accelerate smartly away.

Like most of London's original tube railways, the Central London followed the line of roads above, with the result that where the roads were narrow the general scheme of platforms between the tracks at a common level had to be modified. Thus at Notting Hill Gate and Post Office the westbound track and platform were above the eastbound; the reverse arrangement applied at Chancery Lane.

The white-painted running tunnels were 11 ft. 8¼ in. in diameter, with enlargements as required on curves and at stations. They lay between 60 and 110 ft. below the surface, the greatest depth being in the middle of the line between Notting Hill Gate and Holland Park. The original intention was to have 11 ft. 6 in. diameter tunnels; this measurement allowed for the lining of the iron rings with brick and/or concrete. This lining work was not carried out, except for a few yards at the ends of station platforms. Although the minimum diameter was 11 ft. 6 in. in these short lined sections, the minimum diameter of the rest of the line, measured to the iron work, was 11 ft. 8¼ in., the diameter adopted later for the other London tube railways.

Most of the tunnelling for the original Central London Railway was through the London clay, and, with the use of the Greathead shield, no special difficulties were met. One of the hardest tasks was the building of the Bank station, where a mass of pipe subways had to be diverted. All the pipes were arranged in a special tunnel of their own immediately beneath the public subways, which the Central London had agreed to build and hand over to the City Corporation in return for being allowed to build under the open area at the Bank free of charge.

The steelwork for the booking hall at the Bank was temporarily assembled in a field and was then transferred, section by section, to its site at the Bank. This station is built over the dried-up course of the once-navigable Walbrook.

In 1896 negotiations with the Great Eastern and North London railways over the station at Liverpool Street failed, and it was decided to make the Bank station the terminus, although the tunnels were carried some distance beyond for use as reversing sidings.

In 1897 it became possible to build Davies Street station on the site originally proposed, instead of on an alternative site at the junction of Marylebone Lane and Oxford Street, for which special powers had had to be obtained, and the scheme for the alternative site was dropped. In 1898 things had got to a state when a general manager could be appointed, and Granville Cuningham from the City of Birmingham Tramways joined the new railway.

The line was originally to be worked by trains with locomotives at the head and tail – a forerunner of the multiple-unit principle – but the Board of Trade refused to allow the power lines to be carried through the train (even though this was allowed for the Waterloo & City). Greathead therefore decided on single heavier locomotives capable of hauling seven cars. They were designed somewhat after an American pattern, built for the Baltimore & Ohio, by the company's electrical engineer, Horace Parshall. The locomotives were built in America by the General Electric Company. The cars, much more massive affairs then those of the City & South London, were built by the Ashbury and Brush companies. There were 168 of these cars, each with longitudinal and cross seats for 48 passengers. They were 45 ft. 6 in. long and had straps for standing passengers to hold. They had gates on end platforms, worked by train attendants or conductors as on the C.S.L.R.

The original power station was built on the site of a fine house and garden known as Woodhouse Park, Wood Lane; the train depot was on the same site. The 'generating house' was 200 ft. by 86 ft. and the boiler house 150 ft. by 87 ft. The running shed was 360 ft. long and 160 ft. wide, and the combined car repair and painting shed was also 360 ft. long. There was a shop for locomotive repairs and wheel turning, and a locomotive running shed 140 ft. long.

The Wood Lane power station generated electricity at 5,000V.; it was one of the earliest stations to generate electricity at such a high voltage.

Three of the original substations – Notting Hill Gate, Marble Arch, and Post Office – were located at the bottom of the station lift shafts. This proved a disadvantage so long as rotary converters were in use and these low-level substations were eventually abandoned. It is now feasible, with modern rectifier equipment, to locate substations in lift shafts again, and it could well be said that in their choice of site the designers of the Central London Railway were well ahead of their time.

The substations fed current to the track at 550V. d.c. The track itself had three rails, the running rails being 100 lb. per yd. bridge-type rails on oak longitudinal timbers. Cross timbers carried the 85 lb. per yd. positive conductor rail, which was mounted on porcelain insulators between the running rails.

On 27 June 1900, the formal opening ceremony took place. Among the distinguished company was again the Prince of Wales (later to become King Edward VII) who took a great interest in the new $5\frac{3}{4}$-mile tube line between Shepherd's Bush and the Bank. The company travelled westwards from the Bank, and to quote a contemporary account: 'The electric train, with its seven carriages, glided with an ease that was almost magical out of the brilliantly-lit Bank station into the great tube that has been cut into the London clay . . . slipped through brightly-lighted white-tiled stations one after the other, until, twenty minutes after it had started, it climbed smoothly up into sunlight once more at Shepherd's Bush.'

At the depot the Prince of Wales made the only speech of the day. He said, 'I have great pleasure in declaring the Central London Railway open. I am sure it will prove a great boon to our great City; and I think Sir Benjamin Baker, its engineer, is to be congratulated on the success with which he has carried out the undertaking. I ask you to drink with me success to the Central London Railway.' Possibly the shortest opening speech on record!

As the *Daily News* said a month later: 'When a place is royally opened it is not always really opened'; and it was not until 30 July 1900 that the new stations opened their doors to the public. On that day 84,500 passengers thronged the trains and stations, and thousands more looked on. On 4 August 1900, the *Daily Mail* recorded: 'Meantime London, all agape, crowds to the Twopenny Tube. Thursday's traffic returns completely eclipse the previous day's, as the following list shows; Monday – 83,000 passengers; Tuesday – 91,600 passengers; Wednesday – 86,000 passengers; Thursday – 93,000 passengers.

'Yesterday the crowds swayed and surged to get on to the trains. It was a cosmopolitan throng. Nearly every civilised nation under the sun was represented among the humanity that was struggling to experience London's latest sensation.'

With its flat fare of 2d. and its careful siting to tap a main traffic stream, the Central London may claim to be the line that Londoners took to their hearts. It was the first really modern tube. Its smart trains, hauled by their electric locomotives in crimson lake with gold lining and polished brass-work, opened the eyes of London to the possibilities of underground travel far more than the C.S.L.R. or the Waterloo & City had done. In the five remaining months of 1900 it carried nearly 15 million passengers, running from 05 00 to midnight on weekdays, with a reduced service on Sundays. The route, connecting the residential areas of west London with the City and running the length of Oxford Street to serve the shopping and theatre areas, could scarcely have been better chosen to attract passengers at all times of the day and evening.

It was not long, however, before the Central London ran into trouble. The attractive American-built double-bogie locomotives, with their central cabs, had their armatures built directly on to the axles, obviating gears and making them very silent. Their four motors gave them 800 h.p. (one-hour rating) and a tractive effort at starting of 14,100 lb. Efficient as the system of mounting the motors was, it meant that of the locomotive weight of 43 tons only a quarter was spring-borne, and they set up a vibration which disturbed property owners along the line so much that a Board of Trade committee was set up to investigate.

The Central London Railway co-operated whole-heartedly in the enquiry, which confirmed that there was serious vibration, and three of its locomotives were converted to operate with 150-h.p. geared motors. This reduced the weight to 31 tons, of which 21 tons were spring-borne. The railway also made up two six-car trains with two cars in each train converted to motor cars by fitting them with two 100-h.p. geared motors each, giving 400 h.p. per train. Tests with the geared locomotives showed that the vibration was greatly reduced, but no vibration was noticed at any point on the surface when the multiple-unit trains ran below. As a result of these trials the railway decided to replace the locomotives by 64 motor cars and to make the multiple-unit trains up to seven cars. A new motor giving 125 h.p. was designed for the stock, giving 500 h.p. per train. The service was being fully worked with the new trains by June 1903. The easier turn-round made a two-minute service possible against the 2½-minute service which was the best that could be provided with the locomotives. At first, the motor cars had to be manned by a crew of two, but later, after the adoption of the 'dead man's handle', only a driver was required.

An interesting feature of the locomotives was that they had a series-parallel controller of the drum type made up of a wooden cylinder with the copper segments attached. This drum was no less than 18 in. in diameter and required some physical effort to move it. To assist him with a certain amount of leverage, the driver was provided with a control handle 21 in. in length! After replacement by multiple-unit trains, all but two of the locomotives were scrapped. For a time two of these locomotives were used by J. S. Raworth, after adaptation, to demonstrate his regenerative braking system on the Metropolitan. The trials took place before the first World War.

Just before that war, the two remaining locomotives and 64 motor cars were still in service, and there were also 133 trailers and 38 control trailers. Two 0–6–0 steam locomotives were also used when power was off in the tunnels. Built to tube loading gauge by the Hunslet Engine Co. Ltd. in 1899, these were side-tank locomotives fitted with condensing apparatus. They were oil-fired in the tunnels but coal could be burnt in the open, and a small coal bunker was provided for the purpose. Both steam locomotives were sent for scrapping in 1923. The last of the Central London electric locomotives was in service for shunting purposes until 1942, when it too was withdrawn.

In 1902 a Bill was submitted to Parliament for powers to extend the line from Shepherd's Bush to Hammersmith, Piccadilly, Strand, and the City to form a 'Central London Circle', on which it was proposed to operate a service similar to that provided by the Circle line. The Bill was rejected, and although revived a year or two later, was eventually abandoned; the opening in 1906 of the Great Northern, Piccadilly & Brompton Railway from Hammersmith to Finsbury Park (now part of the Piccadilly Line) had removed most of the original attractions of the scheme.

The Central London was now in a settled form, but from 1905 there was a steady drop in passengers, no doubt largely due to the counter-attractions of the Metropolitan and District railways, which had recently been electrified, and possibly also of the motor bus. In 1907, therefore, it was decided that the twopenny flat fare should not apply to passengers travelling more than seven or eight stations and in July of that year a 3*d*. fare came into force. The 'Twopenny Tube' was a twopenny tube no longer, though the name lingered.

The first extension to the railway came in 1908, when on 14 May, the opening day of the Franco-British Exhibition at the White City, the railway opened a loop line from Shepherd's Bush to Wood Lane. This sharply-curved half-mile line was designed to improve terminal working by eliminating the cross-over at the western end of the line, and a station was built on it near Wood Lane to serve the exhibition. The exhibition brought a rise in traffic, but its closing was marked by another decline. Possibly to compete with the motor buses,

PLATE 16. Stockwell Station on London's first real tube railway, the City & South London, in 1890. One of the locomotives is preserved in the Science Museum at South Kensington, and a car is displayed at the London Transport Museum Covent Garden

PLATE 17. The Prince of Wales (afterwards King Edward VII) at Stockwell station after opening London's first electric tube railway, the City & South London, on 4 November 1890

PLATE 18. Oxford Circus station in early Central London Railway days. Note the large 'TUBE' sign

PLATE 19. Early Central London Railway trailer car showing the typical 'gate' ends

PLATE 20. The Central London Railway carried parcels from 1911 to 1917. This shows activity at Post Office (now St. Paul's) station

PLATE 21. One of the main-line size cars built for the Great Northern & City Railway

PLATE 22. This unusual movable platform extension, which could be swung clear when the depot tracks were in use, was built in 1928 at Wood Lane station to accommodate White City Stadium traffic

PLATE 23. Underground in war-time. Part of the Plessey factory which stretched five miles through the new Central Line tunnels under Eastern Avenue at Wanstead and Ilford. The new tunnels had not been opened for traffic when the 1939–45 war began

PLATE 24. Underground in war-time. Scene at the Bank when a bomb exploded under the station concourse on 11 January 1941. Part of the concourse wall can be seen on the right

PLATE 25. A Piccadilly Line 1959 stock 'silver' tube train in Rayners Lane station

PLATE 26. View from a bridge at Wembley Park, showing 'A' stock Metropolitan Line 'silver' trains to left and right and on the dive-under track leading to Neasden depot. Bakerloo Line tube trains of '1938' stock are on the centre tracks. The double-chimneyed building in the background is Neasden generating station – now demolished

PLATE 27. An 'A' stock Metropolitan Line train leaving Moor Park for Watford

PLATE 28. Interior of an 'A' stock train, Metropolitan Line

PLATE 29. Two of the 30 MW. 50-cycle turbo-alternators at Lots Road

PLATE 30. The main control room at the modernized Lots Road generating station which supplies power for the Underground lines

the Central London introduced a penny fare, for three stations, in 1909.

In 1911 the company started to carry parcels and mails, for which special compartments were provided on the trains. In the compartments rode a parcels porter who sorted the traffic during the journey. A number of tricycle-mounted messenger boys collected the parcels and delivered them; special wicker hampers were used between surface and platform levels. The service lasted until 1917, when the war had reduced the staff to the point where it could no longer be carried on. It was never resumed.

The year 1911 also saw the introduction of season tickets on the line. A short extension at the eastern end carried the Central London from the Bank to Liverpool Street, on 28 July 1912. Parliamentary powers had been obtained for this extension in 1892, but the scheme had been postponed. Four escalators were installed at the new station, two connecting with the Great Eastern station and two with Broad Street (North London Railway). They were of the early 'side-stepping' variety.

The Central London's signalling was mechanical and very much like that on the City & South London, using Spagnoletti's lock-and-block system. There were semaphore starting signals at the platforms, but in the tunnels, where there was less room, the inner and outer home signals were sliding coloured spectacles. Between the Bank and Shepherd's Bush there were 14 signalboxes. These included separate boxes for each direction at the three two-level stations – Post Office, Chancery Lane, and Notting Hill Gate. As on the C.S.L.R., the block section extended from the starting signal at one station to the outer home of the next, the line between the outer home and the starting signal at that station forming a separate section controlled by the signalman at the station concerned. The brush-on-last-bogie system was employed to check that a train had actually passed inside the outer home. There were signalboxes at each terminal station in addition to the 14 mentioned. Track circuits (a.c.) and automatic signals were installed eventually, the work beginning in 1912.

On 1 January 1913, the Central London Railway became a member of the Underground Group of companies.

VIII The Great Northern & City: Metropolitan and District Electrification

THE NEXT TUBE railway to be opened was, and for many years remained, a curious anomaly. It was the Great Northern & City Railway, built in 16-ft. diameter tunnels to take main-line stock and carry Great Northern suburban trains into the City at Moorgate from a connection near Finsbury Park. The southern end of this $3\frac{1}{2}$-mile line – the only main-line size tube in London – is deep below the surface at Moorgate. It ran northwards via Old Street (built as a joint station with the City & South London), Essex Road, Highbury & Islington, and Drayton Park to Finsbury Park, where its station was alongside that used by the Piccadilly Line under the Eastern Region main-line station. The station tunnels were not only of large diameter but built to take full-scale suburban trains. Their platforms were 420 ft. long except at Finsbury Park and Moorgate, where they were 30 ft. longer. The line was built by S. Pearson & Son.

With the building of the Victoria Line, the Great Northern & City section of the Northern Line was truncated to run between Moorgate and Drayton Park only, a connection being given by the Victoria Line between Finsbury Park and Highbury & Islington. One of the former G.N. & City platform tunnels at Finsbury Park is used by the Victoria Line and the other by the Piccadilly Line, giving easy same-level interchange between southbound trains on the two lines. (One of the former Piccadilly Line platforms is used by the Victoria Line, giving easy interchange in the northbound direction also.)

The large cars formed seven-car trains when the line was opened on 14 February 1904, using three motor cars and four trailers. This was true multiple-unit stock, built by the Brush Electrical Engineering Company, but it seems not to have been the first in London, as is sometimes claimed. Even if the Waterloo & City stock was not true multiple-unit stock, there were true multiple-unit trains on the Central London by then.

The G.N. & City motor cars each had two 125 h.p. motors, one for each bogie, geared to the axle. Electrical equipment was supplied by the British Thomson-Houston Company. All cars had end platforms with lattice gates. Traction current came from the railway's own power station at Poole Street, midway along the line, obviating any need for substations. It reached the trains via a four-rail system in which both current rails lay outside the running rails.

The G.N. & City installed an automatic signalling system devised by J. E. Spagnoletti, son of the C. E. Spagnoletti of the Great Western Railway. This apparatus had been tried on part of the Central London Railway, but had not met 'fail-safe' requirements. Each station had outer home, inner home, and starting signals and on leaving a station the train automatically put the starting signal to danger and cleared the two home signals simultaneously. The starting signal was not cleared until the following outer home went to danger. The points at the terminal stations were manually operated. The Board of Trade Inspecting Officer of Railways refused to allow this system to remain in use for more than three months as it was so designed that it could fail in several ways while showing clear signals instead of putting the signals to danger. The apparatus was redesigned by one of Spagnoletti's assistants, A. H. Binyon, with R. P. Brousson, engineer and traffic manager of the line, and in its modified form it was accepted and worked for many years. The G.N. & City, with this apparatus was the first tube railway to have automatic signalling throughout using light signals without moving parts. (There were a few electrically-worked semaphore signals where the line came into the open at Drayton Park.) It was also the first tube railway to have an insulated traction current return.

No extensions to this line were ever made, though it had powers to continue at the southern end to Lothbury and may have hoped to turn itself into a main-line link between north and south London by burrowing under the river. The shops and sheds were built at the side of the station at Drayton Park, where the line comes to the surface. There were hydraulic lifts at the various stations, and there is now an escalator connection with the other underground lines at Moorgate. The line was busy, but it seemed to be stagnating after a while – useful link as it was and still is – and its short independent life ended when it was taken over by the Metropolitan Railway on 1 July 1913. The original rolling stock lived out its full life, but the power station was closed down, the Metropolitan supplying the current from its own station at Neasden through a substation. To get to Neasden for overhaul, the stock had to follow a curious route. There was no rail connection with the Metropolitan at Moorgate, so the stock was dragged up a sloping connection at Drayton Park and taken by steam power over the G.N.R. lines and the Widened Lines to Aldersgate. There it reversed and was hauled over the Metropolitan to Kensington High Street and the District on to Acton Town and Rayners Lane, where it got back on to the Metropolitan and thus to Neasden. This roundabout route from Aldersgate was necessary because the cars were too big to go through the Baker Street–Finchley Road tunnels on the old St. John's Wood line.

The Bakerloo – the Baker Street & Waterloo Railway – was the next tube to open. This was on 10 March 1906, but before going on with tube railway history we must have another look at the two earlier sub-surface railways, on which all the activity with electrified lines was having its effect. To add to the troubles of the Metropolitan and the Metropolitan District, electric trams were spreading and so were mechanically-driven buses. The Central London's short-cut across the Circle line was also a worry to both companies. The Metropolitan had obtained permission to electrify the whole of its lines as far back as 1882 after seeing a small-scale demonstration of electric traction at Wembley Park. The District had given some consideration to battery locomotives in 1888 but decided against them. Now great strides had been made in the technique of electric traction, and both companies got together, as they were both concerned with working the Circle line, and spent £20,000 on a full-scale experiment. They electrified the line from Earl's Court to Kensington High Street on the third-rail system and supplied direct current from a temporary power station at Earl's Court. Each company paid for three coaches of a six-car experimental train which was fitted with Siemens motors.

The experiment went well when it started in February 1900, and passengers were carried on the experimental train from 21 May to 6 November, at first paying 1*s*. each for the privilege. Subsequently the Metropolitan and the District set up a joint committee which recommended that electrification should proceed, using the three-phase 3,000V. a.c. system developed by the firm of Ganz in Hungary. This used an overhead conductor wire system, and the arguments in its favour were much the same as those for a.c. electrification today – no substations would be needed and the overhead wires would be much cheaper than conductor rails. The Metropolitan accepted the findings but the District did not. By then it was under a powerful outside influence – Charles Tyson Yerkes.

The name of Yerkes crops up in many places when London's transport is discussed. He was born in the U.S.A. in 1837 and became a financier and stockbroker at an early age, for he was only in the middle thirties when he was ruined in the financial panic after the Chicago fire of 1871. He then turned to transport and particularly to tramways, and between 1881 and 1899 he managed to secure controlling interests in and unify the tramways of Chicago. At this time Americans were eager to invest in overseas enterprises, and Yerkes, in partnership with others, bought up in 1900 for £100,000 the powers obtained by the Charing Cross, Euston & Hampstead Railway in its Act of 1893. These powers had remained unused because the railway had never been able to raise enough money to put them into effect. The solicitor who dealt with this transaction, R. W. (afterwards Sir Robert) Perks, seems also to have interested Yerkes in the District line. Yerkes was also in the market for the control of the Bakerloo line, which was temporarily in abeyance. Yerkes, aided by Perks, secured control of the District in March 1901 and announced that the line would be electrified and modernized. He also got rid, not too gently, of Forbes, who was still the chairman at that time. Forbes was succeeded for a short while by a stockbroker who had helped in the negotiations – Murray Griffith – but in September 1901 Perks became chairman.

The Yerkes group formed the Metropolitan District Electric Traction Co. Ltd. to electrify the District and build a power station. It was incorporated in July 1901, for Yerkes had wasted no time, and arranged to build the power station to supply not only the District but also the Brompton & Piccadilly Circus tube railway – another proposed line picked up in passing, as it were, by Yerkes. There was so much activity in this direction that on 9 April 1902 the Yerkes group formed the Underground Electric Railways Company of London Ltd., which took over the Metropolitan District Electric Traction Co. Ltd. and arranged to take in hand the building and equipment of the Brompton & Piccadilly Circus, the Charing Cross, Euston & Hampstead, and the Baker Street & Waterloo underground lines already mentioned, and also the Great Northern & Strand. Yerkes became the chairman and remained so until his death in 1905. The underground railways had become the Underground.

The Ganz system of electrification, which had been tried on only one European line, did not suit Yerkes at all. He was familiar with low-voltage d.c. electrification in the U.S.A. and could see it at work in the newly-opened Central London tube which so disturbed the poverty-stricken District. He decided on low-voltage electrification for his tubes and for the District. This decision brought him against the Metropolitan, a powerful opponent, and the question which system should be used went to arbitration. The verdict went to Yerkes, who offered to take over the Metropolitan on lease and was refused. The Metropolitan had no choice but to fall in with the new system.

The electrification was carried out on the District by the American engineer-in-chief and general manager of the Underground Company, James Russell Chapman. As we have already recorded, South Harrow had its first train services on 28 June 1903; these were by District electric trains. This was because the Ealing & South Harrow was equipped early for electric traction and supplied from a temporary generating station at Alperton. A section of the line was opened in connection with one of the Royal Agricultural Society's shows, at Park Royal, on 23 June 1903. This section ran from Mill Hill Park (renamed Acton Town in 1910) to Park Royal, and the service was extended to South Harrow five days later. The whole of the District railway (as it then was) was converted before the end of 1905. The system adopted used third and fourth rails with the positive rail outside the running rails and the negative in the centre. Current was supplied at 600V. d.c. On the Wimbledon line south of Putney bridge, which belonged to the London & South Western, the running rails were later bonded to the negative rail so that that railway's trains, working on the three-rail system, could use the same tracks.

Power came from a huge power station at Lots Road, Chelsea, to which coal could be brought by barge to be unloaded at its water frontages on the Thames and Chelsea Creek. Work had been started on the power station in March 1902, even though more than a year and a half was to pass before the whole site was secured. It went into service on 1 February 1905. Its four great chimneys aroused much controversy at the time, and Whistler, the artist, was one of those most against it. A suggestion from *Punch* that the chimneys should support a large equestrian statue to Thomas Carlyle was perhaps not taken seriously but shows that the dispute was not merely a local one. It was not long, however, before the power station was part of the familiar London scene and artists were painting its reflection in the Thames.

It was built originally to supply the District and, later, the three

Underground Group tube lines, but in the end it was supplying the City & South London, Central London, the East London, parts of the Southern and London, Midland & Scottish Railways, the London United Tramways network, and many other installations such as Acton overhaul works and the London General Omnibus Company's Chiswick Works.

Lots Road has been improved and increased in capacity from time to time but at first it had eight steam turbines each producing about 7,500 h.p. at 1,000 r.p.m. These were each coupled to generators producing three-phase current at 11,000V. 33⅓ cycles.

Allied to the District electrification was the installation of automatic and semi-automatic signalling, controlled by the trains themselves through track circuits, and the introduction of pneumatically-operated points. The whole of the District Railway running track was track-circuited, and most of the sidings and yards. Advantage was taken of this to install illuminated track diagrams, controlled by the track circuits, in signal boxes. These showed the position of every train in the area controlled by the signalbox concerned. This is thought to be one of the earliest large-scale uses of such diagrams.

Every stop signal had an associated 'train-stop', which applied the brakes of any train which ran past a signal at danger. Another feature introduced at this time and thought to have been first used on the District Railway was the train describer apparatus which enabled a signalman to pass the description of a train to the next box and so on all down the line. The describer apparatus was capable of receiving and storing train descriptions and presenting them in the proper sequence to the signalman at the receiving point. The description was cancelled by the train itself, through the track circuits, as it left the platform, allowing the next description to appear on the signalman's panel. Normally, the describer showed the next three trains. The apparatus was also used to work illuminated platform signs showing passengers the destinations of trains.

The electrification of the Metropolitan Railway, with its 'main-line' characteristics, was in some ways more difficult. A power station was built at Neasden on the east bank of the River Brent. It was never as large as the District's power station, which was designed from early days to serve the tube lines as well, and originally had four 1,000 r.p.m. turbines coupled to generators producing three-phase alternating current at 11,000V. 33⅓ cycles. The current was fed by high-voltage lines to substations at Baker Street, Neasden itself,

Harrow-on-the-Hill, Ruislip, Bouverie Street, Moorgate, Chalton Street, and Gloucester Road, and these first eight were followed by others. All had rotary converters to bring the supply down to 600V. d.c. to feed to the rails. The first line to be electrified was that from Baker Street to Uxbridge, on which electric trains ran from 1 January 1905. In July that year the District electrified from Ealing Broadway to Whitechapel, which included the southern half of the Circle. The Metropolitan had electrified its half of the Circle in readiness for through electric running on 1 July 1905, but had adopted a narrower collector shoe than the District. When the service began, it was found that the narrower Metropolitan shoe would not run properly on the less-accurately-laid District track and Metropolitan trains had to be confined to the South Kensington–Aldgate section until wider shoes could be fitted. Through running round the Circle began in the week ended 24 September 1905. Electrification reduced the running time of the Circle trains from 70 to 50 minutes for the round trip.

The electric services on the Metropolitan began with multiple-unit trains, but as the volume of traffic on the then rural sections of the line north of Harrow did not justify electrification – the service at the turn of the century was approximately hourly to Rickmansworth and two-hourly beyond – steam-hauled trains continued. To make the best use of the electrified sections of the line, particularly those in tunnel south of Finchley Road, the Metropolitan decided to introduce electric locomotives to work trains on the in-town section, handing over to steam locomotives at convenient points in the suburbs.

Two batches of ten electric locomotives were built by the Metropolitan Carriage & Wagon Co. The first ten were delivered in 1905–06 and the second batch during 1907–08. The two types differed radically in appearance. Nos. 1–10 were of 'camel-back' or 'steeple cab' design, having a central driving position flanked by a lower equipment compartment at each end. Locomotives Nos. 11–20 were box-like in appearance, with a flat-fronted driving cab at each end and the equipment mounted in the central section on both sides of a central gangway.

When these locomotives were first put to work on Aylesbury line trains, the locomotive change point was at Willesden Green, although electric trains could run to Harrow-on-the-Hill (and Uxbridge). However, on 1 November 1906, facilities for changing locomotives were brought into use at Wembley Park and then at Harrow on 19 July 1908. Electric services were extended on 5 January 1925 to

Rickmansworth, and locomotive changing facilities were provided at that point.

The District also acquired some electric locomotives, mainly to haul London & North Western Outer Circle trains between Earl's Court and Mansion House. There were 10 of these units, built by the Metropolitan Carriage & Wagon Co. and fitted with four 200 h.p. motors each. The electrical equipment was made in the U.S.A. In appearance these 28-ton machines, which normally worked in pairs with coupled controls so that they could be driven by a single driver (multiple-unit operation), were disappointing, looking like bogie vans with clerestory roofs, but they seem to have been quite efficient. When the Outer Circle service was cut back to Earl's Court (1 January 1909) the locomotives were used on the Circle line with one at the back and one at the front of a train of trailer cars – much as Greathead had wanted to do on the Central London. When through trains began to run from Ealing to Southend on 1 June 1910, they were hauled between Ealing and Barking by the electric locomotives. The last five of them were withdrawn in 1939.

The District's new multiple-unit electric stock included gate-platform cars used on the South Harrow line in 1903 and also on the Hounslow branch. The Hounslow line was purchased by the District on 1 July 1903 and became the first District line to be converted for electric running (the South Harrow line had no train service before electrification). Electric services from South Acton to Hounslow Barracks began on 13 June 1905. This was the first time that the South Acton branch had been open to public traffic, though the line had been completed in February 1899 and had been authorized 21 years before that to provide a link with the North & South Western Junction Railway. The trains ran to Hounslow Town station and there reversed to continue over a newly-laid curve to Hounslow Barracks. Hounslow Town was replaced in May 1909 by a new station on the main line, so that trains no longer had to reverse. (Northfields station had opened as Northfield Halt the year before.) The line from Hounslow Town (renamed Hounslow East in 1925) to Hounslow Barracks (renamed Hounslow West) was single-track for some time with one intermediate station called Heston Hounslow (which became Hounslow Central). The single-track was doubled by 1 November 1912 to Heston Hounslow and to Hounslow West by 28 November 1926.

The greater part of the District's new stock, however, was of

American design and made up 60 seven-car trains of three motor cars and four trailers each. All cars were 49 ft. 6½ in. over buffers, 8 ft. 10½ in. wide, and 12 ft. 3¼ in. high from rail level. It was open saloon stock, the two end cars each seating 48 and the intermediate cars, including a power car, each seating 52. The general plan was the same as that used for the cars of the Brooklyn Elevated. All the main electrical equipment was supplied by British Thomson-Houston, but the cars were built partly by British builders and partly on the Continent. This was the Class 'B' stock, the earlier South Harrow stock having been Class 'A'. Classes 'C', 'D', and 'E' were similar and were obtained in 1911, 1912, and 1913 respectively. All these cars except the 'E' type had clerestory roofs. The 'E' type had an elliptical roof with torpedo ventilators: the ventilators were draughty and were soon removed. None of these types survives in passenger service.

There was a gap during war years, and then came the Class 'F' stock of 1920. This had normal elliptical roofs and was of all-steel construction without running boards, enabling it to be some inches wider than previous stock. An unusual feature of the class was the provision of oval-shape windows in the end walls and three double doors on each side, enabling passengers to move very quickly into and out of the cars. The class originally numbered 100 vehicles; the builders were the Metropolitan Carriage & Wagon Company. They were extensively renovated in 1952/53 and most were still running on the Metropolitan Line at the end of 1962. The last 'F' stock train ran on 7 September 1963.

Class 'G' (1923–24) went back to the clerestory roof. All 50 cars were motor cars built by the Gloucester Railway Carriage & Wagon Co. Ltd. Two cars of this class had driving cabs at each end and were used as single cars to work the Acton Town–South Acton branch, as a shuttle service, until the line was closed on 28 February 1959. Fourteen of these cars were converted to trailers in 1959 and were then grouped in the 'Q converted' category. Class 'H' consisted of the original 'B' motor cars converted to trailers and has now disappeared. Class 'K' was designed in 1927 but not delivered until 1929/31. There were 100 motor cars, each 50 ft. long and fitted with built-in 'non-stopping' indicator. They were built by the Birmingham Railway Carriage & Wagon Co. Ltd. and later also became 'Q converted'. They retained the clerestory roof but had some refinements of styling.

The Class 'L' cars were built by the Union Construction & Finance Co. Ltd., a subsidiary of the Underground Group. The class consisted of eight motor cars and 37 trailers and was similar to the 'K' stock. The motor cars subsequently became trailers and the whole class joined the 'Q converted' category. Very similar to the Class 'L' cars were the 11 motor cars and 17 trailers of the 'M' stock built by the Birmingham company in 1935 and also the 26 trailers of Class 'N' built by the Metropolitan-Cammell Carriage & Wagon Co. Ltd. in 1935. The 'M' stock motor cars were converted to trailers, and all cars of both types joined the 'Q converted' stock.

The Metropolitan also needed new electric stock, and it too turned to American-style cars for its inner services. They were of composite steel and timber construction and were 52 ft. 6 in. long over the centrally-placed buffers and automatic couplers. Originally they had open end platforms and gates, but these were soon enclosed. The cars were built by the Metropolitan Carriage & Wagon Company, and the first batch consisted of 56 motor cars, 36 driving trailer cars, and 76 ordinary trailers. The equipment for these was made by the British Westinghouse Company (later the Metropolitan-Vickers Electrical Co. Ltd.). The motor cars had all four axles driven, each by its own 150 h.p. motor. Trains of this stock were usually made up of two three-car sets, each consisting of a motor car, trailer, and driving trailer. In addition, a batch of 26 motor cars was fitted with British Thomson-Houston equipment, 12 having 150 h.p. motors and the rest 200 h.p. motors. The British Westinghouse equipped cars used a low-voltage control system not unlike that used today and well in advance of their time. The B.T.H. control equipment made use of the full line voltage, and the result was that the two types of stock could not be used together. As well as the multiple-unit sets, the Metropolitan had some bogie compartment stock converted for electric working, using both types of equipment.

In 1913, 23 car sets of British Westinghouse equipment were purchased, with traction motors, and 13 of these were fitted to new motor cars built by the Metropolitan Carriage, Wagon and Finance Company. The other 10 sets were used to replace the equipment (B.T.H.) in the second series (Nos. 11–20) of the Metropolitan's electric locomotives. The equipment removed was fitted at the railway's Neasden works into 10 new motor cars.

During 1922 and 1923 the Metropolitan Railway put into service 20 new electric locomotives, numbered 1–20, in place of the original machines. These new units were built by Vickers Limited at Barrow-in-Furness. They were 39 ft. 6 in. long and were mounted on two four-wheeled bogies. Each bogie carried two 300 h.p. nose-suspended motors, four positive current collector shoes – two on each shoe-beam – and two negative shoes – one attached to brackets on each traction motor casing – making eight positive shoes and four negative per locomotive.

There were driving positions at each end of the 'round-nosed' bodies, with the equipment installed in the centre section between communicating gangways down both sides of the locomotive. The equipment included air compressors for the Westinghouse brakes of the locomotive itself and exhausters for vacuum brakes fitted to the passenger stock. As the locomotives were equipped for two different braking systems, they carried two 'trip cocks' on each front right-hand shoe beam.

When delivered, the locomotives were finished in the Metropolitan Railway locomotive livery of maroon with black and straw lining, with red solebars, buffer beams and window frames. The fleet name 'Metropolitan' was carried centrally on the sides, flanked by the Metropolitan coat-of-arms. The locomotive number appeared four times – on each side below the fleet name, and at both ends.

The locomotives, which weighed 61½ tons and had a tractive effort of some 22,000 lb., were designed to accelerate from rest to 25 m.p.h. in 25 seconds and to be capable of a top speed of 65 m.p.h. in order to deal with the frequent closely-spaced stops between Aldgate and Baker Street as well as the long non-stop runs on the outer sections of the Metropolitan. They were also designed to start a 265-ton freight train up a 1 in 45 gradient on straight track and to shunt at speeds as low as 2 m.p.h. Their wheelbase, 29 ft. 6 in., permitted the negotiation of 3 ch. curves.

Contemporary accounts state that the 20 locomotives were rebuilds of the original locomotives of 1905–08, but, as an illustration of the locomotives under construction shows 15 of them in the Vickers works at the same time, this is not possible. In fact, the original idea was to rebuild the locomotives with improved performance, but after a trial locomotive (No. 17) had been dealt with in this way it was decided that the results were not satisfactory. The plan was then abandoned and new locomotives were ordered.

One of the locomotives, No. 15, was shown on the Metropolitan Railway stand at the British Empire Exhibition at Wembley in 1925; for this purpose the panelling on one side was removed to show the interior and equipment.

In 1926 it was decided that the electric locomotives should be named, and the first nameplate appeared on 18 March of the following year. No. 15 eventually became *Wembley 1924* to commemorate the first year of the exhibition, which brought much traffic to the railway. The other 19 locomotives all received names of famous actual or fictitious persons connected with the area served by the Metropolitan – by then so well publicized as 'Metroland' that the name was a household word. The names carried were:

1	*John Lyon*	11	*George Romney*
2	*Oliver Cromwell* (*later Thomas Lord*)	12	*Sarah Siddons*
		13	*Dick Whittington*
3	*Sir Ralph Verney*	14	*Benjamin Disraeli*
4	*Lord Byron*	15	*Wembley 1924*
5	*John Hampden*	16	*Oliver Goldsmith*
6	*William Penn*	17	*Florence Nightingale*
7	*Edmund Burke*	18	*Michael Faraday*
8	*Sherlock Holmes*	19	*John Wycliffe*
9	*John Milton*	20	*Sir Christopher Wren*
10	*William Ewart Gladstone* (*later W. E. Gladstone*)		

The locomotives were rehabilitated after the 1939–45 war, the work starting in 1953. All but one of them, (now used for brake tests), have now been withdrawn, One, *John Hampden*, is preserved in the London Transport Museum. The equipments from the older locomotives were used at Neasden, with the motor bogies and motors, to power motor cars similar to the 1913 stock.

The cars built earlier had clerestory roofs and doors at the centre and ends of the car only; the centre doors had been added after delivery. The 1920/21 stock had three pairs of sliding doors on each side. None of the original Metropolitan open electric stock is now running.

There was another type of Metropolitan electric stock, known from 1938 as 'T' stock. The 'T' stock was made up of compartment vehicles and at one time consisted of 60 driving motor coaches and 97 trailers. These were delivered mostly between 1927 and 1933, but 25 trailer coaches were converted at various times between 1927 and 1941 from older rolling stock built for locomotive haulage.

In 1925 the Metropolitan Railway extended its electric services from Harrow to Rickmansworth and opened, in conjunction with the London & North Eastern Railway, the short branch to Watford. At first the L.N.E.R. shared substantially in the provision of trains, but after the 1926 strike the L.N.E.R. Watford service was not restored. When traffic on the line increased, the Metropolitan agreed to provide more rolling stock.

At that time the Metropolitan Railway had a very mixed fleet of passenger vehicles, much of it 20 or so years old. The inner suburban services were largely provided by the electric multiple-unit saloon type trains and the longer-distance trains (on the Aylesbury service) were of the compartment type with locomotive haulage – electric as far as Rickmansworth and steam beyond.

To provide additional and more powerful motive power, the Metropolitan ordered 12 compartment-type driving motor coaches from the Metropolitan Carriage, Wagon & Finance Co. (later Metro-Cammell Limited), of Birmingham, in 1927. They were generally similar to the 'Dreadnoughts', and each had four Metropolitan Vickers 275 h.p. motors.

In 1930, to cope with increased traffic, the Metropolitan bought 30 more motor coaches and 25 trailers from the Birmingham Railway Carriage & Wagon Co. Ltd., and the final order for this stock went to Birmingham in 1931. It consisted of 18 motor coaches, 14 driving trailers, and 33 trailers.

This multiple-unit compartment stock was used on the services from the City and Baker Street to Rickmansworth, Watford, and to a lesser extent Uxbridge. It was also used on the 4½-mile Stanmore branch from its opening on 10 December 1932 until 20 November 1939, when the Bakerloo Line service took over. The special train for the official opening of the Stanmore branch was a unique formation. Three first-class coaches, the Metropolitan directors' saloon, and one of the two Pullman cars were marshalled between two 1930 motor coaches to carry a special party, including the Minister of Transport and the directors of the company, to the ceremony at Stanmore on 9 December 1932.

The Metropolitan shared the provision of rolling stock for the Hammersmith & City line with the Great Western Railway, but the Metropolitan serviced all the cars. They were open saloon cars made up in sets of three – motor car, trailer, and driving trailer. The motor cars had four 150 h.p. motors.

We have now brought the story of the Metropolitan and District railways up to the formation of the L.P.T.B., mentioning briefly the opening of the two-mile branch from the Metropolitan, half-way between Moor Park and Rickmansworth, to Watford. This branch, with its intermediate station at Croxley Green (now Croxley), was opened on 2 November 1925. The Stanmore branch, also opened in Metropolitan Railway days, led out into almost undeveloped country in the hope of creating its own traffic by enabling Londoners to move out into a district brought within half an hour of Baker Street. The contractors were Walter Scott & Middleton, working under the direct supervision of the Metropolitan's own engineers.

By the end of May 1915 the Metropolitan line from Finchley Road to Wembley Park had been quadrupled throughout to take extra traffic. Extra platforms were built at Willesden Green, Neasden, and Wembley Park for the new fast tracks, but there were no platform faces for these tracks at the other stations. Electric working was extended to Rickmansworth on 5 January 1925, with steam haulage continuing beyond, and further quadrupling was carried out, four tracks being open to Harrow-on-the-Hill on 10 January 1932.

Unfortunately, to carry four tracks south of Finchley Road to Baker Street, where they would have been most valuable, was out of the question because it would have been so expensive. This section of track became more and more congested, and even the closing of the intermediate stations (Swiss Cottage, Marlborough Road, and St. John's Wood) in the morning peak hour did not solve the problem. The Metropolitan therefore proposed to build a deep tube of main-line size, like the G.N. & City, from a point on the main line between Willesden Green and Kilburn to a junction with the Circle line on the west side of Edgware Road station. This plan entailed the rebuilding of Edgware Road station and the provision of sidings. Work started on the station in 1926, and it was given two island platforms with four through platform roads. The new station indicators were prepared, and provision was made for them to announce that the next train would be for Aylesbury and Verney Junction. They were never able to show these destinations, for the line was not built and the bottleneck was not by-passed until the L.P.T.B. extended the Bakerloo line and provided two extra tracks between Baker Street and Finchley Road in that way.

IX The Yerkes Tubes

WE LEFT THE Yerkes forces about to build the Brompton & Piccadilly Circus, the Charing Cross, Euston & Hampstead, the Baker Street & Waterloo, and the Great Northern & Strand. Of these, the Baker Street & Waterloo was the first to be started and the first to be opened. It owed its inception, it is said, to a semi-humorous suggestion by some Westminster businessmen that they should have such a line to take them to Lord's as quickly as possible. Examined in a more serious mood, the scheme proved to have merits.

A Bill was promoted in 1891 and came before a Joint Committee of both Houses in 1892. It became an Act in 1893, and work started in 1898. In 1899 the company promoted a Bill for two extensions – to Paddington, and to Euston as well as a deviation in Lambeth. This Bill failed but another was introduced in 1900 and in that year an Act was secured for the extensions to the Elephant & Castle and to Paddington.

Work started in June 1898 with the erection of a staging in the Thames close to Hungerford Bridge. On this was built a small village of workshops and offices, as well as a power station to give power and light for construction work. From this staging two vertical shafts were sunk into the bed of the river so that excavated material could be taken away by barge. It was also intended to take working material in by the same route. The northbound tunnel was started from this point in February 1899, and the shield began to eat its way slowly – 8 ft. a day – towards Trafalgar Square, reaching the station site there in November. By then the southbound tunnel had been started and some of the station work had been put in hand, including Piccadilly Circus and Baker Street. The stations were to be, from the south (including some later authorizations), Elephant & Castle, Kennington Road, Waterloo, Thames Embankment, Trafalgar Square, Piccadilly Circus, Oxford Circus, Regent's Park, Baker Street, Lisson Grove, Edgware Road, and Paddington. As the railway itself put it in the brochure issued to celebrate its opening, 'the advantages which this line will afford for getting quickly and cheaply from one point of London to another are without parallel. It will link up many of the most important Railway termini, give a connection with twelve other Railway systems, and connect with the vast tramway system of the South of London, thus bringing the Theatres and other places of amusement, as well as the chief shopping centre, within easy reach of outer London and the suburbs'. But this was in the future, and misfortune was to befall the line before that. In 1900 came the Whitaker Wright financial failure, and with it the collapse of the Baker Street & Waterloo's backers, the London & Globe Finance Corporation. Work on the line slowly came to a stop and the sites remained derelict for some months until, as already described, Yerkes came along and bought up the remains.

With the new impetus behind it, work started again in 1902 and tunnelling reached a speed of up to 73 ft. a week. The following year a Bill sought to authorize the leasing of the Baker Street & Waterloo to the Underground Electric Railways Company of London, the new Yerkes company which was formed, as we have seen, partly to construct the new tubes. In 1902 the Brompton & Piccadilly Circus and the Great Northern & Strand companies were merged as the Great Northern, Piccadilly & Brompton Railway. The Bakerloo and Hampstead railways were both merged in the Great Northern, Piccadilly & Brompton in 1910, and the composite company thus formed was named the London Electric Railway.

Meanwhile work on the Baker Street & Waterloo continued. One new practice adopted was to fill the lower part of the tubes with concrete on which the sleepers could rest, the ends of the sleepers being embedded in crushed granite. This helped to reduce vibration. Because the rails had to go down the shafts driven into the river bed they had to be kept short, and no rail on the original line was longer than 36 ft. 5 in. A four-rail system was used, but it was discovered that there was a leakage to earth from the outside positive rail, which was near the cast-iron tunnel lining. This caused difficulties at the large Charing Cross substation, which fed the District tracks as well as those of the Bakerloo, and the solution adopted was to change the polarity of the rails so that the centre rail became positive instead of negative. This change remained until 1917, when the Bakerloo went out to Watford and it was desirable to standardize the current supply. By this time advances in technique had made it possible to overcome the original difficulties.

Automatic signalling with train stops was provided from the start, and there were bare telephone wires along the tunnels. The risk of fire, said the company, was practically non-existent. "The Station Platforms are constructed of concrete and iron, and the Permanent way sleepers of Jarrah, an Australian wood which is non-combustible. The Rolling Stock is built almost entirely of steel, the small quantity of wood used being rendered nonflammable.

"THERE IS A LIGHTED FOOTWAY FROM END TO END OF THE LINE. Special Electric Lamps are placed in the tunnels at intervals of 40 feet. The wires for lighting these lamps are entirely independent of the power cables. The space between the rails has been filled in with cement and granite chippings. Should a train come to a standstill and be unable to proceed, the power current would be at once cut off, and passengers would only have to walk a few hundred yards along an easy and well-lighted footpath to the nearest station."

The lifts had exit gates opened and shut by compressed air, and passengers entered them at one side and left them at the other. The entrance gates were hand-worked. The stations were decorated in different colour schemes at platform level, the idea being that a passenger could recognize his own station by the colour scheme peculiar to it. Externally, the stations were all similar in pattern. They were designed by Leslie W. Green, A.R.I.B.A., in the form of a plinth, the idea being that offices, etc., could be added above this base later on. They were given strength by a steel frame and were faced with glazed blocks in a ruby-red shade. There were no surface buildings at Regent's Park, Trafalgar Square, or Embankment.

The multiple-unit rolling stock was, as already mentioned, nearly all-steel in its construction. It was built in the U.S.A. by the American Car & Foundry Company and sent over in sections for erection in Britain. There were 36 motor cars and 72 trailers formed into three-car sets which could run in six-car trains in peak hours and as three-car trains at others. The cars had end platforms with gates and carried attendants, who were responsible for working the gates at the ends of adjacent cars and calling out the station names. A guard (or conductor) travelled in the first car. He was also trained as a driver (motorman) and was expected to take over if the regular driver became incapacitated for any reason. The conductor had to join the attendants in calling out the station names. The rolling stock depot and repair shops were in an open three-acre site at St. George's Circus, Lambeth, near the southern end of the line. This became known as London Road Depot.

The engineers for the line were Sir Benjamin Baker, Messrs.

Galbraith & Church, and H. H. Dalrymple Hay. The last-named was supervising engineer for the Underground group and the others the consulting engineers. James R. Chapman was responsible for the equipment and was resident engineer. There was also a resident track engineer, W. E. Hanson. The contractors for the main part of the line were Perry & Company.

On 10 March 1906, Sir Edwin Cornwall, M.P., Chairman of the London County Council, opened the main part of the line from Kennington Road to Baker Street, and the stations were opened for public traffic the same day.

The Kennington Road station was almost at once renamed Westminster Bridge Road (it stood at the junction of the two roads), but it was changed again in 1917 to Lambeth North, originally with brackets round the 'North'. The short southern extension of the $3\frac{1}{2}$-mile line, to Elephant & Castle, was opened on 5 August 1906. At the other end of the line the railway reached Lisson Grove (renamed Great Central, apparently at the insistence of Sam – afterwards Sir Sam – Fay of the Great Central and renamed Marylebone in 1917) on 27 March 1907 and Edgware Road on 15 June of the same year. At first there was a 2*d.* flat fare, but traffic fell short of expectations and differential fares were introduced. Whether as a result of this, or not, traffic then steadily increased. The useful portmanteau name of 'Bakerloo' is believed to have originated with 'Quex' of the *Evening News*.

C. T. Yerkes did not live to see the first of his tubes opened, for he died in New York on 29 December 1905, at the age of 68. His place as chairman of the Underground Electric group was taken by Edgar Speyer of Speyer Brothers, associates of Yerkes. Speyer Brothers had managed to secure control of London United Tramways in September 1902, when they were a thorn in the side of the District and were even contemplating a tube line of their own, to be fed by L.U.T. trams, from Hammersmith into central London. They had thus turned the powerful L.U.T. into useful allies instead of rivals.

Perhaps the most astonishing thing to happen as a result of the death of Yerkes was that Sir George Gibb, general manager of the prosperous North Eastern Railway since 1891, gave up that position to become chairman and managing director of the District, and deputy chairman and managing director of the Underground group. It was Gibb who steered the Yerkes tubes into being.

The next of these tubes to come into the picture was the Great

Northern, Piccadilly & Brompton Railway, which has come into the story several times already. It was opened by David Lloyd George, who at that time was President of the Board of Trade, on 15 December 1906. It was then nine miles in length, the longest and some ways the most important of the tube railways yet to be opened. At the time of opening it had an authorized capital of £7,206,000 and it brought the length of Underground group lines in operation to about 22 miles.

The Great Northern, Piccadilly & Brompton Railway was an amalgamation of the Brompton & Piccadilly Circus Railway, authorized in 1897, and the Great Northern & Strand Railway, authorized in 1899. Powers to combine the schemes were obtained in 1902, including the building of a connecting line from Piccadilly Circus to a junction with the Great Northern & Strand at Holborn to give a through route between the two railways. This left part of the Great Northern & Strand between Holborn and the Strand (Aldwych) as a double-track branch line, which it still remains, though only one track is complete and in use.

There were 22 stations (though not all were ready for traffic) when the line was opened: Finsbury Park, Gillespie Road (renamed Arsenal in 1932), Holloway Road, Caledonian Road, York Road (closed in 1932), King's Cross, Russell Square, Holborn, Covent Garden, Leicester Square, Piccadilly Circus, Dover Street (renamed Green Park in 1933), Down Street (closed in 1932), Hyde Park Corner, Knightsbridge, Brompton Road (closed in 1934), South Kensington, Gloucester Road, Earl's Court, Barons Court, and Hammersmith. There was also Strand station (later Aldwych) on the branch. The stations from South Kensington westwards to Hammersmith adjoined those of the District. Between South Kensington and West Kensington the new tube ran under the District Railway and in fact formed part of the District's deep-level tube, authorized in 1897 but never built, apart from this smaller-scale version and a short length of tunnel at South Kensington, now disused.

The engineers for the line were Sir J. Wolfe Barry, C. A. Brereton, Sir James W. Szlumper, W. W. Szlumper, and Alexander Ross. The engineer-in-chief of the Underground Electric Railways Company, James R. Chapman, was responsible for everything concerned with the equipment. The engineer concerned with the tunnelling was H. H. Dalrymple Hay. The contractors were Walker, Price & Reeves; Walter Scott & Middleton; and Bott & Stennett. The last-named firm did the work on the open-air section. Work started in April 1902 on the Holborn–South Kensington section, and three months later the South Kensington–Earl's Court section was in hand. The Finsbury Park–Holborn section was started in September of the same year, but the line west of Earl's Court was not begun until February 1904.

The station tunnels were 21 ft. 2½ in. diameter; at some stations they had to be built above one another to keep within the width of the road above. At South Kensington, for example, there is an 18-ft. difference in level. Generally, however, the tunnels were built side by side, with the stairways, lift shafts, etc., between them. Above ground, the stations followed the general style of those built for the Bakerloo, with flat roofs for later vertical extension. Finsbury Park station was built by the Great Northern Railway and leased to the tube line.

The depth of the tubes below ground level varied from 20 ft. at Finsbury Park to 123 ft. at Covent Garden. Electric lifts were used at most stations to carry passengers to and from the street; in all, 60 lifts were installed in 18 stations. Gillespie Road station, where the railway was close to the surface, had no lifts, and at Finsbury Park two hydraulic lifts were provided for the use of passengers interchanging with the Great Northern Railway, which, being on a viaduct at this point, was a considerable distance above the tube railway. There were two similar lifts for interchange between the G.N. & City and the G.N.R. There was an interesting experiment at Holloway Road station in the form of a double spiral escalator (up and down) moving at 100 ft. per minute. This was installed in one of the lift shafts and was apparently in good working order a week before the official opening of the railway; but for reasons now uncertain it never went into public service. This was five years before the first passenger escalator was opened, also on the Piccadilly Line, at Earl's Court in 1911. The Holloway Road escalator was still there in 1919.

Construction work made such good progress during the second half of 1906 that the company decided, possibly to secure traffic from Christmas shoppers, to open the railway before the stations at Covent Garden, Down Street, and South Kensington, and the Strand branch, were finished. Arrangements were made with the contractors for the line to be opened for public traffic before being officially handed over to the railway as completed.

The opening ceremony, as already stated, was duly performed on 15 December 1906, and the service started with 26 three-car trains giving a 3-minute headway in peak periods. Fares ranged in ½*d.* stages from 1*d.* to 3*d.*, with a 4*d.* fare for the whole of the nine-mile journey, which took 38 minutes. As new cars were delivered by the makers, trains were increased in length to six cars. On the Aldwych branch, the standard train was of two cars. (The branch was opened on 30 November 1907).

Rolling stock was supplied by two continental companies, one French – Les Ateliers de Construction du Nord de la France (Blanc Misseron) – and the other Hungarian – The Hungarian Railway Carriage & Machinery Works (Raab), Hungary; each built 36 motor cars, each seating 46 passengers, and 72 trailers, seating 52. There were also two British cars, supplied by the Brush Electric & Manufacturing Company Ltd. and the Metropolitan Railway Carriage & Wagon Co. Ltd. The entire fleet of 218 cars was made up of all-steel gate-ended stock, similar to that used on the Baker Street & Waterloo Railway. Two of the French-built cars lasted until July 1956, their half-century of life being due largely to the fact that for many years they provided the Aldwych shuttle service.

A depot and car sheds were provided at Lillie Bridge on a site formerly occupied by the sheds, repair shops, and yards of the District Railway before that company opened its depot at Mill Hill Park (now known as Ealing Common depot). The only access the Great Northern, Piccadilly & Brompton Railway had to its own depot was across District Railway tracks. The signalling arrangements, track, safety devices, lifts, etc., followed the same lines as on the Baker Street & Waterloo, except that the current-rail polarity was not reversed.

In July 1910 the Great Northern, Piccadilly & Brompton was renamed the London Electric Railway, as already mentioned, having absorbed the Bakerloo and Hampstead lines.

The last of the tube lines to be opened was the Charing Cross, Euston & Hampstead Railway, incorporated in 1893. Its publicity referred to it openly as 'The Last Link' in the London tube network. The Act of 24 August 1893 empowered the company to build a tube railway from Charing Cross (at the corner of Southampton Street and the Strand) to Heath Street, Hampstead. A branch from this line to Euston would end at Chalton Street, St. Pancras. The company secured additional powers to buy land by an Act of 1894, gained an extension of time by an Act of 1897, and by another Act of 1898 gained permission to divert the Charing Cross end of the line to a terminus in Craven Street instead of Southampton Street. The next year another Act authorized a one-mile branch from Camden Town to Kentish Town station on the Midland Railway and a deviation to bring Euston on to the main line. A further extension of time was secured by an Act of 1900. All this procedure in Parliament had a slightly academic flavour, for the company was quite unable to raise the money to do any building, even though the 1897 Act gave power to pay interest out of capital during the time the line was being built.

All this was changed when on 1 October 1900, as we have seen, Charles Tyson Yerkes bought up the powers for the Hampstead tube.

There is a story that Yerkes and H. H. Dalrymple Hay, the engineer (afterwards Sir Harley Hugh Dalrymple Hay), drove in the Yerkes private hansom cab along the route of the tube which Yerkes had acquired. Starting from Charing Cross they went all the way out to Hampstead Heath, and then Yerkes decided to drive on. They went through the fields to Golders Green cross-roads, open and empty, and Yerkes declared that there was where his line would end. Powers for the extension to Golders Green and for the main line from Kentish Town to Highgate (Archway Tavern) were secured under an Act of 1902. This was not, however, the whole story. On that same day another Act received the Royal Assent. This was for the Edgware & Hampstead Railway, originally controlled by a separate company but brought into the Underground Group fold. The directors were replaced by Yerkes nominees in January 1903. This Act was for a railway 4½ miles long from Golders Green to Hendon and Edgware. In the following year another Act incorporated the Watford & Edgware Railway Company, to build another six miles of railway and complete the link with Watford. Although the Underground got to Watford, it was in a different way, as we shall see presently.

Work on the original part of the line started in September 1903. There were to be stations at Charing Cross (Strand), Leicester Square, Oxford Street (now Tottenham Court Road), Tottenham Court Road (now Goodge Street), Euston Road (now Warren Street), Euston, Mornington Crescent, Camden Town, and then – the line having divided – Chalk Farm, Belsize Park, Hampstead, and Golders Green on the main line and South Kentish Town (now closed), Kentish Town, Tufnell Park, and Highgate (now Archway) on the branch.

The line was the work of Sir Douglas Fox & Partners and W. R. Galbraith as consulting engineers, and the tunnel work was carried out under their direction with A. W. Donaldson as resident engineer. The engineer who had ridden with Yerkes to Golders Green, H. H. Dalrymple Hay, supervised the work for the Underground Group and also acted as engineer for the construction of Charing Cross station (of which more later). He had J. C. Martin with him as resident engineer. The architect for station buildings was Leslie W. Green, and James R. Chapman, the Underground Group's chief engineer, was responsible for the whole of the permanent way and equipment, the surface portion of the railway at Golders Green, and the erection and equipment of the car sheds and repair shops at Golders Green. W. E. Hanson was resident engineer for the permanent way work, and Gilbert Rosenbusch superintended the installation of the lifts.

All the equipment was very similar to that used on the Bakerloo and Piccadilly Lines, and there was no special novelty in the contruction of the tunnels and permanent way. The only tunnelling difficulties met with were at Euston, where water-bearing sand was struck and work had to be done under compressed air. The quicksand was not a very bad one, however, and a comparatively low pressure proved enough to keep it out of the workings. The contractors were Price & Reeves.

Where the line did differ from the others was in its depth below ground in places because of the rising country through which it ran. There is a 272 ft. rise between Charing Cross and the tunnel mouth south of Golders Green station. The deepest point below the surface is about 300 yd. north of Hampstead station, where the rails are 250 ft. below the crest of Hampstead Heath. Hampstead station itself, where there are now high-speed lifts, is 192 ft. below ground. The shallowest station, Chalk Farm, less than $1\frac{1}{2}$ miles away, is 42 ft. down. Another unusual feature was the station at North End, Hampstead, better known as the 'Bull and Bush'. This does not appear in the list of stations already given because, although the station tunnels and part of the station below ground were duly built, nothing was ever done at street level and no access could be gained except by rail. The rail-level facilities are sometimes used for storage.

The stations were again designed as plinths for taller structures, each consisting of a ground and mezzanine floor and framed in steel. The most difficult station was Charing Cross (later Strand, to distinguish it from the District, Circle, Northern, and Bakerloo station on the Embankment). This station was at one time to have been on the northern side of the Strand, but the South Eastern Railway eventually agreed to its being built under the forecourt of the main-line station, where interchange would be easier. The South Eastern stipulated, however, that the surface of the forecourt must not be broken, so that the cab services which brought their passengers to the trains would not be interrupted. This made things difficult, but the Hampstead engineers prepared to dig upwards from the running tunnels until they reached the booking-hall floor level and build the sub-surface facilities in this way. As it happened, however, this topsy-turvy procedure was not required. On 5 December 1905 part of the roof of the South Eastern station collapsed, killing six people and destroying the Avenue Theatre next door. (The present Playhouse theatre, used by the B.B.C., replaced the Avenue in 1907.) This tragedy caused the main-line station to be closed for 3½ months and the cab traffic, of course, also stopped. In the circumstances the South Eastern agreed to the Hampstead's having permission, for six weeks, to dig in the forecourt. Work started in January 1906, and before the six weeks were up one shaft was fully excavated and the walls of the booking hall were 12 ft. down from the surface. At this stage the steel beams for the roof, supporting the station forecourt, were put in place and the surface was restored. The rest of the work was done under cover, the spoil being dropped down the shaft and carried away by rail. Those who watched the widening of the Strand in recent years may be surprised to hear that the entrance to Strand station was aligned with the new building line – half a century before.

The station platforms were built, like those of the Piccadilly line, 350 ft. long. (The Bakerloo, having started earlier, had only 291-ft. platforms.) These platforms were served by five-car trains made up of two motor cars and three trailers. The total fleet, at the start, consisted of 60 motor cars, 50 control trailers, and 40 trailers. They were built by the American Car & Foundry Company and assembled at Trafford Park, Manchester. During peak hours they ran a two-minute service between Charing Cross and Camden Town, with a four-minute service on each of the two branches. The fare for the whole distance was 3*d.*, with 2*d.*, 1½*d.*, and 1*d.* fares for shorter distances. The power supply came as, with all the Yerkes lines, from Lots Road.

The line was opened on 22 June 1907, by David Lloyd George. It was a Saturday, and the line was thrown open for the rest of the day for free travel by Londoners: 140,000 of them took the opportunity.

X The Underground Grows

THE YERKES pattern was now complete, and the main Underground network of Central London was in very much its present shape. All the lines had extensive interchange facilities, and London had the finest underground railway service that could then be imagined. It was generally assumed that no more needed to be done.

In July 1907 the London Passenger Traffic Conference was established with Gibb as its chairman and, indeed, as its originator. Its object was to co-ordinate the working of all the underground railways of London, whether in the Underground Group or not. The conference agreed, in December 1907, to use a distinctive symbol at all stations. This symbol was the well-known 'UNDERGROUND', with large initial and last letters. In a slightly amended form it is still used by London Transport today. The equally well-known bull's-eye or roundel sign owes its origin to a device adopted by the London General Omnibus Company in 1905, which incorporated a wheel across which was a bar bearing the word GENERAL. Its first appearance for railway use was in 1909 as a solid red disc behind station names, and in 1913 with the word UNDERGROUND, with large first and last letters, across the middle.

Also in 1907, just before the conference was formed, a new personality arrived on the London scene. Albert Henry Stanley had been born, as Albert Knattriess, in Derby in 1874, but his family went to the United States when he was still very young and his father changed their surname to Stanley. He started his transport career very humbly with the Detroit Street Railway Company but rose rapidly to become assistant general manager, Street Railway Department, Public Service Corporation of New Jersey, in the autumn of 1903. In February 1904 he became manager, and less than three years later he was general manager of the Corporation. Soon after this he was invited to become general manager of the Underground group and he took over in the Spring of 1907. Sir George Gibb evidently had him marked, for when Gibb retired at the end of 1910 Stanley was made managing director of the Underground Company also. Stanley was to be responsible for shaping London Transport into its unified form and for initiating important developments to the system. He was knighted in 1914, entered the Government in December 1916 and became President of the Board of Trade. He returned to the Underground Group as its chairman in August 1919. He was created Baron Ashfield of Southwell in 1920 and was the first chairman of the London Passenger Transport Board when it was created in 1933. He retained the chairmanship almost to the end of the Board's life, resigning from 31 October 1947, having been appointed a member of the British Transport Commission in August. He died in 1948.

But all this was still well in the future. As from 1 July 1910, the London Electric Railway had been formed, and it sought powers to build an extension of the Hampstead tube southwards from the Strand terminus to a point underneath the District Railway's Charing Cross station on the Embankment. One of the objects was to provide direct interchange between the Bakerloo, District, and Hampstead lines. The work was authorized by an Act of 1911, and a loop line was built with a single platform under Charing Cross (District) station. (This is the present northbound Northern Line platform.) It was opened on 6 April 1914. The name of the station on the Embankment became Charing Cross (Embankment) and that of the Strand station Charing Cross (Strand). On 9 May 1915 the names of Charing Cross and Strand were substituted.

Powers had been obtained in 1912 for the L.E.R. to take over the authorized but unbuilt Edgware & Hampstead Railway. Nothing could be done during the 1914–18 war, but work was started on 12 June 1922 on the Golders Green–Hendon section. This line was on the surface and had one intermediate station at Brent. It was opened on 19 November 1923. Work on the Hendon–Edgware extension started at once, but as this three-mile line includes a half-mile tunnel section it took longer to build and was not opened until 18 August 1924. The tunnels, known as the Burroughs tunnels, are of standard tube-tunnel dimensions. There are two intermediate stations on the line – Colindale and Burnt Oak. Stations of a style in conformity with their (then) rural surroundings were designed by S. A. Heaps, architect to the Underground Group. The platforms were 350 ft. long and of the island type. The consulting engineer for the Edgware extension was Sir Harley H. Dalrymple Hay and the consulting architects were Adams, Holden & Pearson. The contractors were Charles Brand & Son and The Foundation Co. Ltd.

A new car shed was built alongside the station at Edgware with accommodation for 28 cars. It was needed because new stock was being obtained for the Edgware extension and also for the link made with the City & South London Railway, now to be described.

When the City & South London passed into the hands of the Underground Group in 1913 one of the first things to be done was to promote a Bill for the enlargement of the tunnels to the then standard tube diameter of 11 ft. 8¼ in. These powers were granted the same year, and the L.E.R. also obtained powers to build a connecting link from Euston to the Hampstead line at Camden Town. The war held up the scheme, but during 1915 the C.S.L.R. power station at Stockwell was closed down and power was fed from Lots Road.

Not much could be done immediately after the war, and the C.S.L.R. found itself short of nearly everything. Shortage of staff and rolling stock were two main troubles, so to improve running in the peak hours the railway installed automatic signalling. Reconstruction of the line was made much easier by the new signalling.

Reconstruction work began on 9 August 1922, when the line between Moorgate and Euston was closed completely. Work started on the same day on the Moorgate–Clapham Common section, but here work was done only at night, whereas on the other section it went on round the clock. For most of the length it was possible to enlarge the 10 ft. 6 in. tunnels by putting in four new segment pieces to enlarge the tunnel and make it effectively 11 ft. 8¼ in. in diameter, even if of a slightly irregular shape. The remaining 10 ft. 2 in. tunnels, between Borough Junction and the Elephant, were rebuilt with new segments. As the rolling stock of the line was small, a shield was designed for the cutting work which allowed trains room to pass through it during the day. On the 11 ft. 6 in. part of the tunnels (Borough Junction to Moorgate) no shield was used and most of the lower segments were not moved. The Moorgate–Euston section was undertaken by Perry & Co. (Bow) Ltd., and Charles Brand Ltd. The rest was done by the railway's own staff, with contract labour for mining supplied by Walter Scott & Middleton Ltd. Single-line working was instituted between Stockwell and London Bridge, but this gave only a skeleton service (the line had been closing at 8 p.m. every night in any case) and after a roof fall where Newington Causeway crossed the railway on 27 November 1923, it was decided to close the line completely from 28 November 1923. Work then went on continuously, and the opportunity was taken of making many other improvements which could not have been done under traffic. The Moorgate–Euston section was re-opened, and the Camden Town connection with the Hampstead line, built by John Mowlem & Co. Ltd., opened, on 20 April 1924. A through service was at once begun between Moorgate and Golders Green.

The Moorgate–Clapham Common section of the C.S.L.R. was re-opened on 1 December 1924. The work on the line as a whole had entailed not only tunnel enlargement but the installation of the standard fourth-rail system and automatic signalling of the type used on the other Underground lines, as well as the replacement of the locomotive-hauled stock by multiple-unit trains. The station tunnels had also been lengthened to 350 ft. and the stations had been modernized.

While this work was going on, powers had been granted in December 1923 to extend the line from Clapham to Morden. This extension was opened on 13 September 1926, with intermediate stations at Clapham South, Balham, Trinity Road (now Tooting Bec), Tooting Broadway, Colliers Wood, and South Wimbledon.

Under an Act of 1923, powers had been obtained to build an extension, two miles in length, of the Hampstead line from its Charing Cross terminus to Kennington, where it would have a junction and interchange station with the C.S.L.R. Work started on this line on 22 April 1924, and it was brought into use, with an intermediate station at Waterloo, on 13 September 1926. (The old Charing Cross loop was closed on 25 January 1926, Highgate trains being turned for the time being at Strand, and Golders Green and Edgware trains using the single platform at Charing Cross, running through the one tunnel in both directions.) The consulting engineers for the Morden extension were Mott, Hay & Anderson; the contractors were Charles Brand & Son and the Foundation Co. Ltd. For the Kennington connection the consulting engineer was Sir Harley H. Dalrymple Hay and the contractor the Metropolitan Tunnel & Public Works Co. Ltd.

The only other piece of construction work on this line before the London Passenger Transport Board took over was a short single-track connecting line between the eastbound Piccadilly and the northbound City & South London line at King's Cross, opened on 1 March 1927. This was built to enable stock to be run to Acton Works for overhaul. The former C.S.L.R. and Hampstead lines were now one, and after running through a series of names, of which the Morden–Edgware was the most persistent, it eventually became the Northern Line of London Transport.

We must now bring the story of the various lines up to date. When the LPTB took over all the Underground railways on 1 July 1933 (except the Waterloo & City) planning on a broad scale became possible. Together with the London & North Eastern and Great Western Railways, the LPTB embarked on a great programme of New Works, with assistance from the Government – this was a time of depression, and the scheme was in part a means of providing employment.

The 1935–40 New Works Programme, often called the £40 million plan, affected the Highgate branch of the Northern Line. It was proposed to build a new extension from Highgate to East Finchley (L.N.E.R.), electrify the L.N.E.R. lines to High Barnet and Edgware, and build an extension from Edgware to Aldenham with intermediate stations at Brockley Hill and Elstree. The former Great Northern & City line, renamed the Northern City line in 1934, was to be linked with the Great Northern by building a new link at Finsbury Park and electrifying the L.N.E.R. line from Finsbury Park to East Finchley and also the L.N.E.R. Alexandra Palace branch.

The two-mile tube extension from Highgate to East Finchley was opened on 3 July 1939, and on 14 April 1940 tube trains of the Northern Line were extended over electrified L.N.E.R. tracks to High Barnet. Before any of this had been done, the original Highgate station on the tube line had its name changed to Archway (Highgate). This was in readiness for the opening on 19 January 1941 of the new Highgate tube station, beneath the L.N.E.R. station. On 18 May 1941, when the 1939–45 war was of course well in progress, tube trains were extended from Finchley Central over a single electrified L.N.E.R. track to Mill Hill East. After the war, in changed circumstances and with Green Belt proposals in mind, the remainder of the scheme was abandoned, including a certain amount of civil engineering work already done for the Aldenham extension. The well-advanced rolling stock depot at Aldenham became eventually the nucleus of London Transport's present bus overhaul works. Had the line been completed, the station at Aldenham, in deference to local wishes, would have been re-named 'Bushey Heath'.

We left the Bakerloo at Edgware Road in 1907 contemplating an extension to Paddington; but by 1909 it was felt that the original proposal would put the station at Paddington in such an unfavourable position that further extension would be impossible, and the scheme was dropped. Later, more ambitious plans were prepared for extending the railway to the north-west, and on 1 December 1913 an extension was opened to Paddington on a line which allowed the tracks to turn northwards, and on 31 January 1915 they had reached Kilburn Park via Warwick Avenue. (Maida Vale station was opened on 6 June the same year.) On 10 May the same year through running over London & North Western Railways track was introduced to Willesden Junction, the Bakerloo being the first London tube railway to be connected physically with a true main-line railway. On 16 April 1917 through running was extended to Watford Junction, five years before the L. & N.W.R. itself began its Euston–Watford electric service. That remained the extent of the Bakerloo Line for more than 20 years.

The rolling stock used for the through services to Watford was unusual in that it was a joint design of the L.E.R. and L. & N.W.R. and painted in the latter company's livery. Different platform heights on the two railways led to the adoption of a compromise height for the floor level, 4½ in. above that of other tube stock. Delivery of these cars was delayed by war conditions, and for three years use was made of older 'gate' stock to which detachable raised steps were added to give the required height at platform level.

There was no further change in the extent of the Bakerloo Line before the LPTB was formed in 1933, but there were other important changes. Escalators were installed at various stations; the District Line station at Charing Cross was rebuilt; and in 1928 the opening of the reconstructed Piccadilly Circus station – a new departure in railway architecture carried out on an unprecedented scale – brought greatly improved conditions for Bakerloo and Piccadilly Line passengers using that station. The work also sent Eros into exile in Victoria Embankment Gardens for six years until the station was finished. After the opening of the Underground central overhaul works at Acton in 1922, the overhaul of Bakerloo stock was transferred there from London Road.

The unification of London's underground railways made it possible for the Bakerloo to serve a purpose which its promoters could never have envisaged – to relieve the Metropolitan Line bottleneck between Baker Street and Finchley Road. On 20 November 1939 a new section of tube tunnel between these points enabled the Bakerloo service to be projected northwards over one pair of former Metropolitan tracks to Wembley Park and Stanmore, and the Metropolitan local service between Baker Street and Stanmore to be withdrawn.

Another result was that routine maintenance of the rolling stock was transferred to the recently enlarged Metropolitan Line depot at Neasden, together with the staff. Before the opening of this new extension, it had been necessary to run Bakerloo stock to Acton works (for overhaul purposes) via Willesden Junction, the West London Railway to Earl's Court, and thence over District Line metals to Acton. The new physical connection with the Metropolitan Line provided a more direct route via Rayners Lane. A sequel to this was that it became necessary to reverse the whole of the Bakerloo stock so that cars would enter the works facing the same way as the remainder of the Underground stock. This was achieved during one week-end by running the entire fleet of Bakerloo trains round the Croxley Green (Colne Junction) triangle near Watford High Street.

No major developments took place on the Piccadilly Line for two decades after it had swallowed up the Bakerloo and Hampstead tubes in 1910 and became the L.E.R. Then an ambitious scheme was launched, the chief features of which were the extension of the railway northwards from Finsbury Park to Cockfosters (7½ miles), the four-tracking of the 4½ mile section of the District Railway from Hammersmith to Northfields to allow through running of Piccadilly trains over District metals to Hounslow and South Harrow, and a comprehensive programme of station enlargement and improvement.

Construction work on the extensions, which was begun in the autumn of 1930, proceeded so rapidly that Piccadilly trains were working through to South Harrow by 4 July 1932. The leasing and reconditioning by the Underground company of the Southern Railway's disused viaduct alongside District Railway tracks between Hammersmith and Turnham Green, together with four-tracking of the District Railway beyond this point, enabled Piccadilly Line trains to run non-stop between Hammersmith and Acton Town, a distinctive feature of the line which still exists today. Piccadilly Line trains use the middle two of the four tracks, leaving the remaining two tracks for District Line trains serving intermediate stations. The generous provision of burrowing and flying junctions virtually eliminated conflicting train movements on this section. At the same time, the line was laid out for 40 trains an hour on each track.

On the Hounslow branch, Northfields was reached by Piccadilly Line trains on 9 January 1933 and Hounslow West two months later, on 13 March. Northwards from Finsbury Park, the line reached Arnos Grove on 19 September 1932. The line was open to Enfield

PLATE 31. A 'drum-digger' shield being hauled through a station tunnel at Green Park after completing a Victoria Line running tunnel drive from Victoria. The same shield then took up the running tunnel drive again towards Oxford Circus

PLATE 32. A Victoria-bound, automatically-driven train entering Seven Sisters station on the Victoria Line

PLATE 33. Artist's impression of Oxford Circus station below ground, enlarged and reconstructed to serve the Victoria as well as the Central and Bakerloo lines

PLATE 34. Automatic fare collection at Green Park station. The four-door gates remained open as long as valid tickets were inserted, but closed if a passenger attempted to pass through without a ticket. The system has since been simplified

Plate 35. Battery locomotive hauling train of wagons loaded with conductor rails passing the control tower at Northumberland Park

Plate 36. Her Majesty the Queen buying a ticket at Green Park station on 7 March 1969, when she opened the Warren Street – Victoria section of the Victoria Line

PLATE 37. The ticket hall and four-door type automatic fare collection gates at Brixton, the southern terminus of the Victoria Line

PLATE 38. Three Underground lines, buses, and main-line railways exchange passengers at Victoria

PLATE 39. Platform at Pimlico with one of the motifs, different for each Victoria Line station, behind the seat. Passengers are helped by the repetition of the station name and 'Way out' signs all along the platform

PLATE 40. Coburg Street Control Room, from which the Victoria and Northern Lines are regulated. This photograph shows the Northern Line panels.

PLATE 41. C.69 stock for the Hammersmith & City and Circle Lines in service at Euston Square. The cars have four double doors on each side to allow rapid passenger movement

PLATE 42. Part of the new construction at South Kensington Station where escalators have been installed to give easier interchange between the Circle and District Lines, and the Piccadilly Line

PLATE 43. A specially-built train for handling and carrying long-welded rails demonstrating the unloading of a 300-ft. rail

PLATE 44. One of the gas-turbine power plants installed at London Transport's Greenwich generating station

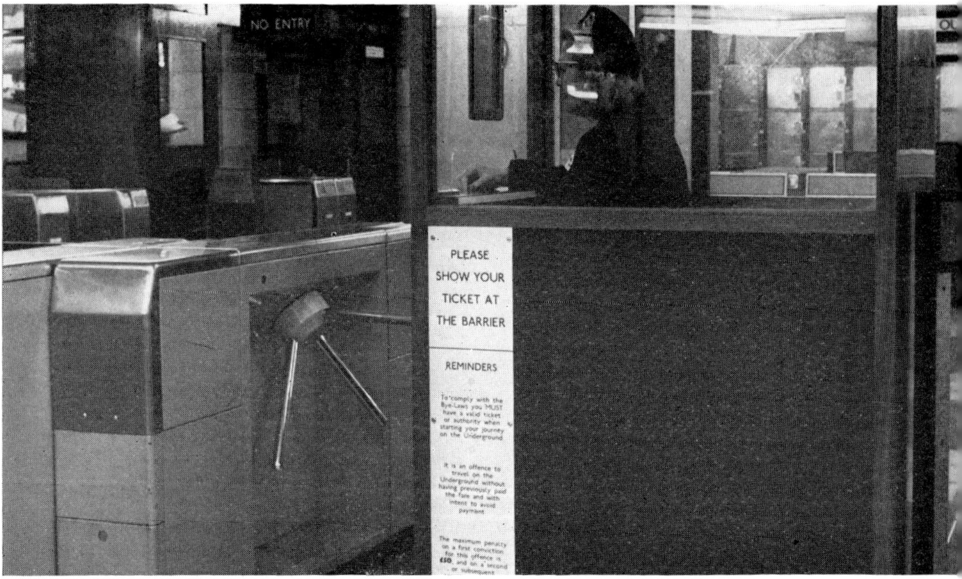

PLATE 45. Pedal-operated tripod gate used for inwards passenger control at Leicester Square

PLATE 46. One car of the Tunnel Cleaning Train, waiting to be marshalled into the complete 5-car unit

West (now Oakwood) by 13 March 1933, and the remainder of the northern extension to Cockfosters was opened on 31 July 1933 (after the undertaking had passed to the London Passenger Transport Board on the first day of that month). The following autumn saw the final extension of the service westwards, when through running began to Uxbridge on 23 October.

The result of these works was a general speeding up of the services, so that, to take only one example, the 38-minute Hammersmith–Finsbury Park run of 1906 was taking 10 minutes less in 1932. Under the same new works programme, stations at Leicester Square, Hyde Park Corner, Knightsbridge, and Holborn were reconstructed – some of them on the Piccadilly Circus pattern, with booking halls below the road surface and numerous entrances from adjacent pavements. Escalators replaced the lifts. In the period 1932–34 a general review of the station facilities on the Piccadilly Line resulted in three stations being closed (Down Street, York Road, and Brompton Road), one renamed (Gillespie Road to Arsenal), and one (Dover Street) modernized with a sub-surface booking hall in Piccadilly and renamed Green Park.

XI The Central London Expands

WHEN WE LEFT the Central London on 1 January 1913, it had just become part of the Underground Group, but already in 1911 the railway had obtained powers to make a connection north of Wood Lane with an authorized Great Western line and to run over it to Ealing Broadway. The Ealing & Shepherd's Bush Railway, as the extension was originally called, had been started in 1913, held up by the war, and used for G.W.R. freight traffic from 1917. It was not until 3 August 1920 that the extension was opened with an intermediate station at East Acton. Two additional intermediate stations, North Acton and West Acton, were opened in 1923. This extension entailed no extraordinary engineering work. The section from the Central London boundary, near Wood Lane, to North Acton was quadrupled in 1938 so that the Underground and main line services were segregated in readiness for the extension of Central trains to West Ruislip.

In 1920, for the Ealing extension, 24 new cars were added to the railway's stock. Most of them had been used temporarily for the Watford through trains of the Bakerloo from 1917 onwards.

In 1928 an unusual platform extension was built at Wood Lane. The opening of the White City stadium had increased traffic at the station to such an extent that demands for extra platform space had to be met somehow, but Platform No. 1, which was used for most of the traffic, was too near the turn-out from the main line to the car depot to be lengthened in the ordinary way, and a movable wooden platform extension was specially designed and built. Normally it continued the line of the rest of the platform, but when the points were to be set for the depot the platform extension, controlled from the signalbox, was swung clear of the points.

In 1947 Wood Lane station was replaced by a modern station named White City on a nearby site, and the old station with its movable platform was no longer needed. At the same time the terminal loop which had been used for many years to reverse the trains at Wood Lane was taken out of use.

There were no further extensions until after the formation of the

LPTB, but a scheme to build a connection from Shepherd's Bush to the London & South Western Railway at Gunnersbury, for which Parliamentary powers had been obtained in 1913, was revived in 1920. The proposal then was to build a link from Shepherd's Bush on the Central London to the L. & S.W.R. west of that railway's derelict Shepherd's Bush station. The object of the 1913 scheme – to get Central London trains through to Richmond – would then be achieved by running powers over the L. & S.W.R. lines via Grove Road (Hammersmith) and Turnham Green. Special arrangements would have been necessary for current supply because much of the line to Richmond was electrified on the fourth-rail system and the C.L.R. was still using a centre third-rail arrangement. Although this scheme was supported by the L. & S.W.R., and powers were obtained, it was never carried out.

Although the length of the line remained static, many improvements were carried out, including the rebuilding of Bond Street station with escalators and the installation of escalators at many other stations. The Central London's power station at Wood Lane was closed in 1928; power then came from the station at Lots Road.

With the formation of the London Passenger Transport Board in 1933 came the establishment of the standing Joint Committee of the Board and the main-line railway companies, the recommendations of which led to the 1935–40 New Works Programme, backed by a £40 million Government guarantee, as already mentioned. The programme included extensions of the Central London, which had been renamed the Central Line in August 1937. Among the works were some to be undertaken jointly by London Transport and the London & North Eastern Railway in east and north-east London and some in west London with the Great Western Railway.

The Central Line was to be projected to connect with the L.N.E.R. Loughton branch line and the Grange Hill loop, which were to be electrified and resignalled. The line was to be extended from Liverpool Street, rising to sub-surface level at Mile End for cross-platform interchange with the District Line and to the surface at Stratford for cross-platform interchange with the L.N.E.R. At Leyton the Central Line was to take over the L.N.E.R. Loughton line. North of Leytonstone part of the service was to run over L.N.E.R. tracks to Loughton, Epping, and Ongar and the northern side of the Grange Hill loop, and the remainder by new tube tunnels along the line of Eastern Avenue to Newbury Park, where it would join the southern half of the Grange Hill loop. In the west, the Central Line was to be extended from North Acton to West Ruislip along new tracks built by the G.W.R. An essential part of the programme was the electrification of the L.N.E.R. main line from Liverpool Street to Shenfield and from Fenchurch Street to Stratford.

The original section of the Central Line had to be improved to give the better clearances needed by larger, faster trains, and platforms had to be lengthened. All this had to be done in the short night hours when no trains were running. Work started in 1938, and one by one many of the tunnel segments were taken out. Packings were then inserted to increase the diameter, and the segments were put back. Some 10,000 rings of tunnel lining were dealt with in this way in two years. At the height of the work gangs were busy in the small hours at nearly 30 points at a time.

The lengthening of platforms was complicated by the gradients up to and down from stations which were a feature of the original line and the fact that the lengthened platforms would sometimes extend to and beyond the point at which the gradient started. The remedy was to steepen the gradients and build the larger station tunnel round the existing tunnel, removing the segments of the running tunnel when the outer work was complete.

The original bridge rails carried on longitudinal timbers set in concrete had to be replaced by bullhead rails carried on normal transverse sleepers. This work had been started in 1913 but was stopped during the 1914–18 war. It was restarted in 1922 and continued at intervals, but two-thirds of the track remained to be rebuilt during the tunnel enlargement programme, completed in 1939. During the tunnel re-aligning operation the original central third-rail system was converted to the standard four-rail system, the final changeover being made in a single week-end. This enabled standard-type tube stock to replace the original stock of 1900.

The eastern extensions of the Central Line gave more than usual difficulty as far as tunnelling was concerned, for it was through a variety of soils calling for different approaches from that needed for the familiar London clay. In driving the shields through the water-bearing strata of the Roding Valley, and through the Lea Valley marshes beyond Mile End, the air pressure in the tunnels had to be raised – sometimes to twice normal atmospheric pressure – to keep the water out of the workings. This entailed the provision of air locks through which men and material had to pass, slowing down the work.

In other places, where soil was loose, a pilot tunnel had to be driven ahead of the main shield. From this tunnel, pipes were driven upwards and a solidifying solution was pumped through them into the ground, making a solid 'roof' layer below which tunnelling could go on. This method was used at the approach to Mile End, where the Central Line rises to sub-surface level to give easy interchange with the District Line. In another place, a river bed had to be hardened by similar methods to let the tunnel pass just below, and the ground beneath the L.N.E.R. Loughton Branch Junction signalbox was similarly consolidated. At that point the top of the eastbound tunnel was only 4 ft. below the foundations of the signalbox.

In other places – beyond Redbridge station, for example – the line came so near the surface that 'cut-and-cover' construction had to be used.

To speed up the work, large numbers of Greathead shields and some rotary shields were used simultaneously, and at one time 40 different sections of tunnel were being built at once. The section of tube line between Newbury Park and Gants Hill is lined with reinforced concrete rings instead of the more usual cast-iron rings.

The western extension from North Acton to West Ruislip was, in general, constructed by the Great Western Railway, London Transport being responsible for the equipment of the line. The works involved the widening of the cuttings and embankments of the Great Western main-line route to High Wycombe and Birmingham and the construction or lengthening of numerous bridges. Some of the new bridges were provided to obviate flat crossings of existing railway tracks and sidings.

New rolling stock depots were being built at Ruislip and Hainault (although White City continued in use), and there were many new stations. Among the most notable of the stations is that at Gants Hill, where the escalators take the passengers down to a lofty hall with platforms each side. The high roof, which is made up of arched segments supported by columns, is similar in constructional character to those of the Moscow Metro.

Another station structure of special note is the covered forecourt for interchange between road and rail services at Newbury Park. This striking building, designed for London Transport by Oliver Hill, F.R.I.B.A., gained the Festival of Britain award for architectural merit, presented by the Council for Architectural Town Planning and Building Research in 1951.

At Greenford station, on the western section, where the platforms are high above street level, an escalator was installed to take passengers up the 33 ft. to the platforms. This was the first occasion on which an escalator had been provided to carry passengers up from street level to London Transport trains rather than down in the usual way.

The 1935–40 New Works Programme had made good progress when the 1939–45 war started, but it then had to be curtailed, slowed down, and eventually stopped. By the time the works were halted, much of the tunnelling from Liverpool Street to Stratford, Stratford to Leyton, and Leytonstone to Newbury Park had been completed. The sections of new tunnel did not lie idle. They were quickly adapted for use as air-raid shelters, bombproof stores, and war material factories. Down to this time, Arthur R. Cooper and then V. A. M. Robertson, successive chief civil engineers of the LPTB, had been responsible for the Board's constructional works.

After the war, London Transport was authorized to continue with the Central Line work, recognized as urgent. War-time equipment was removed and the line was opened to Stratford on 4 December 1946. The Board's chief engineer was now P. Croom-Johnson. Central Line trains reached Leytonstone on 5 May 1947, Greenford (in the west) on 30 June 1947, and Woodford on 14 December 1947. The south side of the Grange Hill loop, now known as the Hainault loop, was opened to Newbury Park on 14 December 1947, on the same day as the Woodford opening, and the east side to Hainault on 31 May 1948. The north side of the loop to Hainault was opened on 21 November of the same year, when the service was extended also to Loughton. On the same day the extension to West Ruislip at the western end was brought into use. Since 1946, more than 29 miles had been added to the Central Line, and this was not the end, for the section from Loughton to Epping was opened on 25 September 1949. The route mileage was then 45 miles, and through trains from West Ruislip to Epping had a run of over 34 miles.

The section between Epping and Ongar was still worked by steam trains, but the electrification of this 6-mile line was started in 1956, and a shuttle service of electric trains took over from steam on 18 November 1957, carrying the Central Line into the heart of rural Essex.

When the major extensions of the 1935–40 New Works Programme were started, it was evident that large numbers of extra cars would be required for the service. Unlike the other tube lines, the original Central Line stations, as reconstructed, and those on its extensions could take eight-car trains, giving a greater passenger capacity. New seven-car trains of what is now known as the 1938 Tube stock were ordered for the Bakerloo and Northern Lines, which have only seven-car trains. On these new trains, all equipment was placed beneath the floor, instead of in equipment compartments as in the earlier motor cars, thus giving about 15 per cent extra passenger capacity. On the Central Line, which was intended to have eight-car trains, the equipment compartments were then less of a handicap; so the displaced Bakerloo and Northern Line cars were earmarked for the Central Line and stored in depots at various points on the Underground system until they should be needed. No less than 1,121 cars of the 1938 stock had been delivered by the time the war broke out – the greatest series of rolling stock replacement orders ever known for an underground railway system up to that time.

When the war stopped work on the extensions, the depots were used for war purposes, and the Central Line stock had to be taken out and stored in the open for some years. Although visited regularly for maintenance purposes, the cars inevitably deteriorated and before being taken into use on the Central Line some hundreds of them had to be passed through London Transport's Acton Works to be brought back into serviceable condition.

We have followed the story of the Central Line to post-war years in order to give a less confusing picture; now we must go back to the Metropolitan, which also had its part in the New Works Programme.

XII Metropolitan Changes: The Post Office Railway

WHEN THE Great Central came at last to London it brought main-line trains on to the Metropolitan Railway, and on 2 April 1906 the whole line from south of Harrow-on-the-Hill northwards, including the branch to Chesham, was transferred to the Metropolitan & Great Central Joint Committee. The trains themselves continued to be provided by the individual companies. The line stayed under joint administration even after the formation of the LPTB in 1933 and remained so until nationalization in 1948.

After the formation of the LPTB it became apparent that the Metropolitan tracks were becoming inadequate for the combination of local and fast passenger trains, and also freight trains, which were using it. Even the advertisements for 'Metroland', which had made such an impression on the London public, were cut down in recognition of the fact that too many more travellers by the line would make things difficult.

Parliamentary powers were obtained in 1935 to widen the Metropolitan Line from two to four tracks from Harrow-on-the-Hill (to which station the line had been quadrupled in 1932) out to Rickmansworth, and also at Chorleywood. It was also decided to electrify the tracks onwards from Rickmansworth to Amersham and Chesham.

All the necessary land was acquired before the war, and a considerable portion of the earthworks was carried out. Steelwork for most of the additional bridges was fabricated and delivered, but work had to stop in the autumn of 1939.

The extension of the Bakerloo to Stanmore has already been mentioned, but it should be said that the original idea was to have one intermediate station, to be called Acacia Road, between the Bakerloo's Baker Street station and Finchley Road. Eventually, however, it was decided to build new stations at St. John's Wood and Swiss Cottage and to close the corresponding Metropolitan stations and also Marlborough Road. (The new St. John's Wood station lay between the Metropolitan St. John's Wood and Marlborough Road.)

The Metropolitan St. John's Wood was renamed Lords for a while and kept open, but it was finally closed on 20 November 1939, when the Bakerloo trains started to work to Stanmore. Marlborough Road was closed on the same day, but Swiss Cottage (Metropolitan) lingered until 18 August 1940. Finchley Road was rebuilt with two island platforms, the Metropolitan trains using the two outer tracks and the Bakerloo trains the inner, thus giving cross-platform interchange between the two lines.

On the Inner Circle, King's Cross station was rebuilt west of the earlier site and nearer the tube station. The new station was in tunnel and was finished in 'tube' style. It was opened on 14 March 1941, the steam trains of the L.N.E.R. and L.M.S. to Moorgate continuing to use the 'widened lines' platforms at the old station.

Before the Metropolitan fades into war and then into nationalization, let us go back for a moment to what Sir Edward Watkin in 1874 had described to Metropolitan shareholders as 'your great terminus' – often nowadays assumed to be Baker Street station but more probably Moorgate Street station, where earlier in the same year he had suggested the erection of a 100-bedroom hotel and shops. Trains of four main-line railways at that time used Moorgate Street station, as well as the Metropolitan.

In 1874 Baker Street was no more than the junction of the single-track St. John's Wood line and the Inner Circle – not then a complete circle, anyway. Today it might well be called a great station, serving the Metropolitan, Circle, Hammersmith & City, and Bakerloo lines and being at once a terminus and a through station – though not on the Manchester–Dover route. It formed when rebuilt – a task which was started in 1912 and went on for many years – a headquarters worthy of the Metropolitan. Chiltern Court, built over Baker Street station and opened in the autumn of 1929, has over 1,000 rooms in its many flats. The Metropolitan always had an eye to the estates part of its business, and the many lands it had had to buy to get its line through northwards were turned to good account as the nucleus of 'Metro-land'. Through a subsidiary company formed in 1919 and called Metropolitan Railway Country Estates Limited, the railway proceeded to develop its own housing estates and actually to design houses and have them built for sale. Before the war, something like 4,600 houses had been built in this way on sites ranging from close to London, like Neasden, to far on the fringes at Chalfont and Amersham.

Before we leave the inter-war years we must look briefly at another type of Tube railway in London. Atmospheric and pneumatic traction for passenger traffic have been mentioned earlier in this book but in 1861 the Pneumatic Despatch Company laid an experimental line about two-thirds of a mile long in Battersea Park. The line consisted of a 2 ft. 6 in. diameter tube in which a small carrier ran on rails. The air in front of the carrier, which fitted the tube closely, was exhausted by a fan and the atmospheric pressure on the rear of the car drove it along like a piston in a cylinder. This line was transferred from Battersea Park to Euston and was laid between the main line station and the North Western District Post Office. It began to carry mail in February 1863. It seemed to have been quite successful and the company, therefore, projected a larger tube, 4 ft. 6 in. in diameter, which would run from Euston to the General Post Office in St. Martins-le-Grand. The line was opened in November 1865 from Euston to No. 245 Holborn, and on the opening day, the Duke of Buckingham, Chairman of the Pneumatic Despatch Company, rode in one of the 'D' shaped cars through the tunnels. He was accompanied by as many others as could cram themselves into the cars. The company talked hopefully of building these tubes between the 10 district post offices and the General Post Office, between main-line termini, etc. The St. Martins-le-Grand extension was duly opened but the line was not a success. Not only did it not pay, but there were technical difficulties, including especially the leakage of air past the carriers.

Nevertheless, the idea of a postal railway must have remained alive in the Post Office, for in 1909, the Postmaster-General set up a Departmental Committee to consider methods of carrying mail in London to avoid delays caused by street congestion and fog; the Committee recommended that a narrow-gauge railway resembling the Chicago narrow-gauge freight tunnel system should be built and that the trains should be automatic, without drivers.

The recommendations were accepted and the scheme was authorized by the Post Office (London) Railway Act of 1913. It was decided that there would be eight stations: Paddington District Office, Western Parcels Office, Western District Office, West Central District Office, Mount Pleasant, King Edward Building, Liverpool Street station, and the Eastern District Office. Extensions were envisaged at the time but not built.

A contract was placed for the tunnel work in 1914 and in the same year a short section of track was built on Plumstead Marshes for experimental work. This had to be suspended during the 1914–18 war but the tunnels were completed and were used to store valuable museum exhibits for the rest of the war. At the end of the war prices had risen so steeply that the whole scheme was revised to see whether the equipment could be made less complex and less expensive. The new scheme was completed in 1923; tenders were sent out and the contracts were placed the next year. In December 1927 the staff had been trained and the line was opened.

It was 6.44 miles in length and of 2 ft. gauge. The double-track is laid in a single 9 ft. tunnel except at the station approaches, where the tracks are separated into 7 ft. tunnels. The current supply is by centre third rail at 440V. d.c. and the return is by one of the running rails bonded at intervals to an earth cable and to the tunnel lining. Both running rails are insulated, the other being used for track circuiting purposes. It is these track circuits which enable the trains to run automatically. A train passing to a new section operates the track circuit on that section and this automatically cuts off the traction current in the section behind.

An extension was made to the railway much later when the Western District Office was moved to a new site in Rathbone Place. The work, carried out under authority of the Post Office (Site & Railway Act) of 1954, was completed in 1958.

XIII The Second World War

ON 1 SEPTEMBER 1939, the Government took control, by an order under the Emergency Powers (Defence) Act, 1939, of London Transport and the main-line railways. This control was exercised through the Railway Executive Committee. Frank Pick, Vice-Chairman of the LPTB, was a member until he retired, when Lord Ashfield took his place. The financial arrangements provided for fixed payments to be made annually to the undertakings taken over, London Transport's share being £4,835,705. Most of the troops in Britain, including many Commonwealth and Allied troops, had to pass through London on their various occasions, especially when transferring from one main-line terminus to another, and many spent periods of leave in the capital. This created a very busy traffic, under difficulties, for London Transport, which was still carrying a considerable load of business travel despite evacuation schemes. A special form of ticket, costing 1*s*., gave forces personnel on leave the freedom of most of London Transport's bus, tram, trolleybus, and Underground services for a day, starting from 10 30. This proved an immensely popular facility.

On London Transport's road services, a cut of about a quarter in fuel supplies meant that services had to be reduced. The number of standing passengers in buses was increased from five to eight, and later twelve. The Green Line coaches vanished from the streets to be converted to ambulances. All this threw further loads on the Underground. At many stations special arrangements were made to keep cycles while their owners travelled to work and back by Underground. At some interchange stations snack trolleys were provided for the forces.

With the weight of the air attacks on London it is not surprising that London Transport's installations received a considerable amount of damage, but the tube stations were regarded immediately by the public as places of safety and they were invaded by hosts of people seeking shelter – so much so that the ordinary and essential business of running the train service became difficult. Sheltering in tube stations had to be controlled, and in conjunction with local authorities and the Ministry of Home Security 79 stations were fitted with bunks, clinics, and sanitary arrangements. Special trains delivered food supplies to 124 canteens throughout the system. In the worst of the early 'blitz' the Underground was carrying its normal load – and more – during the day and sheltering 177,000 every night. Another 17,000 sheltered in tunnels not in use or stations closed to traffic. Special offices were fitted up in disused passages and on platforms at Down Street, Dover Street, Hyde Park Corner, Knightsbridge, and Holborn stations. The Down Street offices were used by the Railway Executive Committee and often by the War Cabinet. Another disused station accommodated the headquarters of Anti-Aircraft Control. The railways themselves had to be prepared, too, with duplicate control systems, emergency repair squads, duplicate power sources, and so on. To minimize the danger of flooding in the tunnels near the Thames, isolating doors were built in subways leading to platforms and in some places in the running tunnels themselves. At Waterloo (Bakerloo and Northern Lines), Charing Cross (Bakerloo), and Strand (Northern), ten electrically-operated floodgates were provided which could close off the tunnels at short notice – less than one minute: these gates weighed nearly 10 tons each. At Charing Cross also, six sector gates isolating the passages leading from the District and Circle Lines to the Northern Line were installed: these weighed $4\frac{1}{2}$ tons each and could also be closed in one minute. As an additional precaution, equipment for erecting steel diaphragms at ten points at Waterloo and Trafalgar Square on the Bakerloo Line, and Waterloo, Charing Cross, and Strand on the Northern Line was provided. Precautions of a similar nature were taken where the City arm of the Northern Line passes beneath the river. These special precautions against flooding required some suspension of services while they were installed. The Strand-Kennington section of the Northern Line was closed for more than three months and the London Bridge–Moorgate section for more than eight months. Concrete plugs were inserted in the tunnels and subways until the floodgates were completed, as they had been at the time of the Munich crisis. Precautions against flooding from broken water mains and sewers were taken at many other stations. On the East London line, vertical-lift floodgates were provided at the south end of the Thames Tunnel, and there were other floodgates along the District Line – at Charing Cross and westwards as far as South Kensington – to protect the line if the Victoria Embankment were to be damaged. Hydrophones in the river picked up the sound of the impact of mines or unexploded bombs and relayed them to the Chief Engineer's control centre. The operation of floodgates, which were manned night and day, was ordered from a control centre at Leicester Square.

All London Transport trains had to be fitted with special reduced lighting for use on open sections of track, and luxuries had to go. The two Pullman cars on the Metropolitan Line were withdrawn to increase the capacity of the trains on 7 October 1939, and on 1 February 1940, first-class accommodation was withdrawn from Metropolitan and District Line trains (except for through trains to the Aylesbury and Watford joint lines).

On 17 May 1940, Frank Pick retired. He had been one of Sir George Gibb's men, assistant managing director of the Underground companies, and then Vice-Chairman of the LPTB. Excellent transport administrator and business man as he was, he will be best remembered for his influence on London Transport architecture, typography, posters, and design generally. He and Lord Ashfield laid the foundations of what might be called the London Transport tradition of design – except that tradition suggests an inability to change.

On 25 June 1940, the first Central London 'alert' was sounded, but no bombs fell. It was the first warning of what was to come, and a few days later direction signs which might have helped an enemy force started to disappear. London Transport's Local Defence Volunteer (afterwards Home Guard) unit had been established on 28 May 1940, and on 21 July it was inspected by the Chairman, Lord Ashfield.

The first bombs on Central London were dropped on the night of 24/25 August 1940; from then onwards London had air raids nearly every night until the end of 1940 and at widening intervals afterwards. On the night of 7 September 1940, tube stations were used as shelters for the first time – a practice which was to continue in greater or lesser degree until 7 May 1945. The Aldwych branch of the Piccadilly from Holborn was closed on 21 September 1940 and it stayed closed throughout the war, re-opening on 1 July 1946. Many British Museum treasures, including the Elgin Marbles, spent the war in the Aldwych branch tunnels.

Now the damage from bombs began. On the evening of 14 October 1940, London Transport's headquarters at 55 Broadway received a direct hit. On the same night a bomb went through the tunnel at Balham station. This was a disaster of magnitude, aggravated by flooding from water mains and sewage. Sixty-eight people lost their lives, and it was three months before the through train service could be restored. A week later the service from Edgware Road to Addison Road had to be suspended because of bomb damage; it was never resumed. On 12 November the recently rebuilt station at Sloane Square, which had been opened on 27 March 1940, was destroyed, but fortunately the conduit carrying the West Bourne over the station was not broken.

The shelterers were now better organized. Catering services for them started on 29 October and were in full operation by 10 December. (They remained in being until 3 May 1945.) The shelterers were given season tickets for their places on 2 November, and the first of thousands of three-tier bunks, eventually to accommodate 22,000 shelterers, at deep Tube stations were installed at Lambeth North on 25 November. In the same month the conversion of part of the new Central Line tunnels under Eastern Avenue at Wanstead and Ilford, as yet unused, was undertaken. This became a large and useful aircraft component factory employing 2,000 workers on day and night shifts. Operated by the Plessey Company, its 300,000 sq. ft. of floor area stretched along nearly five miles of tunnel. Life for the shelterers at the 79 tube stations used for the purpose was made as pleasant as possible. The idea was that six people should occupy six feet of platform space – three in the bunks and three on the platform. The platforms were marked with two white lines, one eight feet and one four feet from the edge. No one was allowed to take shelter before 16 00, but after 16 00 shelterers could occupy the space up to 8 ft. from the platform edge and after 19 30 they could use the space up to the 4 ft. line. The tube stations were not entirely safe, despite their obvious attractions as shelters – at Bounds Green on 13 October 1940, 19 people were killed and 52 injured when a bomb caused part of the station tunnel to cave in, and the day before seven people were killed at Trafalgar Square. The Balham incident has already been mentioned.

One of the worst incidents was at the Bank station on 11 January 1941, when a bomb caused the entire roadway to collapse into the subways and concourse underneath. The bomb burst in the escalator machine room under the concourse itself, injured people on the platforms, and blew the windows out of two trains standing in the station. It also wrecked the escalators. Fifty-six people were killed and 69 injured. The huge crater – 120 ft. long and 100 ft. wide – where the roadway had been was bridged by the Army to let road traffic continue, and temporary stairs were built at one side of the escalator tunnel to enable the station to get back into service. It was, however, closed for over two months. The Central line platforms did not close but passengers had to use the Northern line lifts and booking hall.

As far back as October 1940, the Government had decided that a system of deep shelters should be built in case of intensive bombing. Eight shelters were to be built by London Transport as agents for the Minister of Home Security and they were to have, in all, sleeping accommodation for 64,000 people. Originally it was decided to have ten shelters, each consisting of two parallel 1,400 ft. tunnels, 16 ft. 6 in. in diameter. The sites were chosen so that the tunnels could form part of possible express underground railways in the future. There were five sites south of the river – at Clapham South, Clapham Common, Clapham North, Stockwell, and Oval, and five north of the Thames at St. Paul's, Chancery Lane, Goodge Street, Camden Town, and Belsize Park. The shelter at Oval had to be abandoned because there was too much water in the ground and that at St. Paul's was not built because an Act was discovered which prohibited the construction of works of this nature near the Cathedral. Each of the eight shelters built had two decks for sleeping reached by separate spiral staircases in the access shafts. For a long time they were used for military purposes – one became General Eisenhower's headquarters before D-day – but five of them were opened to the public for a while when the flying bomb attacks started.

On 13 June 1944 the first 'V1' flying bomb fell in southern England. No less than 149 of these were to fall on London Transport premises before the last V1 bombs fell at Sidcup and Waltham Cross on 28 March of the next year. One of the earliest incidents was within a few days of the start of the attack when extensive damage was done to the viaducts carrying the District and Piccadilly tracks between Hammersmith and Ravenscourt Park. The train services were restored, at slow speed, the next day, but two days later another V1 came down in almost the same spot and did further damage to the tracks. It was six weeks before the speed restriction could be removed. The first of the 'V2' rockets fell in the London area on 8 September 1944, and the last on 27 March 1945.

Now the cleaning-up operation could start. The special precautions were relaxed, and equipment was gradually removed. 'VE' day came on 8 May 1945, the last of the bunks vanished from the stations, escalators began to run 'down' again all day (many 'down' escalators had been stopped in off-peak hours during the war to economize in fuel). Victory Day came on 8 June 1946.

There were other sides to London Transport's war effort, however. The workshops of London Transport were mobilized for war purposes in addition to their normal tasks. Examples of the work done by the rail and road shops include the making of more than a quarter of a million of four types of parts for tanks and armoured fighting vehicles and the overhaul and modification of more than 500 armoured fighting vehicles. London Transport workshops were also particularly active in building aircraft – Halifax bombers. A London Aircraft Production Group was formed – four-fifths of its staff without previous engineering experience and more than half of them women. The first aircraft built by the group, of which London Transport was the co-ordinating centre, was flying in 14 months, and by the middle of 1944 more than 500 aircraft had been turned out.

The building department, apart from its work on many adapted buildings, etc., made parts for bridges – deck panels, landing ramps, and bridging pontoons (as well as a tank for float-testing the pontoons).

A voluntary part-time work factory for aircraft components was established on 15 June 1942, in the long, wide subway leading to the exhibition halls at Earl's Court. This continued in being until 14 June 1945.

London Transport staff also lent a hand in the Battle of Britain. It was essential to keep the few aircraft of 'The Few' flying, and London Transport released 400 men for work mainly at the maintenance unit repairing shot-up Hurricanes.

In all this it is impossible to separate the railway and road sides of London Transport. Between them, among many other things, the shops produced 158,000 2 in. shells and 8,000 gun forgings, 80,000 sea mine components, 102,000 road vehicle parts, 37,000 blanks for grenade dischargers. They machined 20,000 gun components, parts for tanks, gun mountings, and sights. They overhauled and tested landing craft motors, rebuilt railway wagons, made parts for excavating machines, fitted up bridge-laying tanks, and waterproofed tanks so that they could operate in 10 ft. of water as they splashed ashore on the Normandy beaches. They rebuilt railway coaches, and they converted railway coaches. They did anything and everything that was asked of them until the war was over.

XIV The Post-war Years

WITH THE END of the war came the inevitable period of taking stock and planning at various levels. At Government level it was decided that the railways and other inland transport facilities should be nationalized, and with them the London Passenger Transport Board. A Transport Bill was introduced in November 1946, and in August 1947 it received the Royal Assent. Vesting day was 1 January 1948, and on that day the British Transport Commission, formed under the Act, took over all the railway and canal undertakings (including the LPTB) which were included in a schedule to the Act. This included all the major railways and joint committees and all the smaller lines which had been under the control of the war-time Railway Executive Committee. Also taken over were the long-distance road haulage undertakings, certain major canals, and hotels and docks which had been associated particularly with the railways.

To assist the Commission in the discharge of its functions a number of Executives were formed, one of which was the London Transport Executive. The London Transport Executive took over, on behalf of the Commission, the undertaking of the London Passenger Transport Board and, in addition, certain joint railway lines. The Met. & G.C. Joint line was divided, London Transport taking over from Harrow-on-the-Hill to south of Aylesbury station, British Railways Aylesbury station and the line beyond to Verney Junction. London Transport also became solely responsible for the Chesham branch and for the Watford branch. In the west it took over the Ealing & Shepherd's Bush line (but not Ealing Broadway station) and part of the Great Western which formed some of the western extension of the Central Line as far as Greenford, but not Greenford station. Also into the London Transport fold came the London & North Eastern Railway lines on which London Transport trains were providing the service through the Central and Northern Line extensions, the East London line from Shoreditch to New Cross (but not New Cross and New Cross Gate stations), the Hammersmith & City Line from Hammersmith to Westbourne Park (but not Westbourne Park station) and the Whitechapel & Bow Railway from Whitechapel to Bow Road.

We have already dealt with the post-war work on the tube lines; but the District, which had only a small share in the 1935–49 New Works Programme, must be dealt with here. The District was allowed to reconstruct some of its stations in the central area, including Earl's Court, Sloane Square, Monument, and Aldgate East. (We have already seen what happened to the reconstructed Sloane Square station during the war.) The work at Aldgate East deserves special mention.

As can be seen from the Underground map, there is a triangle at Aldgate of which, if the Circle Line be counted as the base, the Metropolitan Line from the northern half of the Inner Circle towards Whitechapel forms the left-hand side and the District Line from the southern side of the Circle towards Whitechapel forms the right-hand side. This triangle caused delays to traffic because, so long as its sides could take only six-car trains, the eight-car trains which the traffic demanded fouled the points when they were standing on the triangle and caused delays to other traffic. The remedy chosen was to rebuild Aldgate East station farther to the east, beyond the triangle, and to alter the north and south curves to enable eight-car trains to be accommodated between the junctions. The track had to be lowered considerably to get enough headroom for two ticket halls beneath Whitechapel Road and this had to be done without interference to road traffic above and while the trains continued to run. The method adopted was to leave the existing track at its original level, except for a slight lowering to make room for new girders to support the roadway above, and to build the new station round them. The tracks were supported on wooden staging as the earth was cut away below them. When all was ready, more than a quarter of a mile of track was lowered into its new position in a single day – and in places it had to be lowered 7 ft. Nearly 1,000 men worked on this unusual weekend task. The new station was opened on 31 October 1938.

The District and Metropolitan also had their share of new rolling stock under the pre-war programme. A radically new type of car appeared between 1937 and 1939 to replace all the older District and Metropolitan stock (except the 'long-distance' Metropolitan). This was the 'O', 'P', and 'Q' stock built by Birmingham and Gloucester to London Transport requirements. The 'O' and 'P' stock went to the Hammersmith & City and Metropolitan – 262 motor cars and 103 trailers – and the 'Q' stock – 25 motor cars and 180 trailers – went to the District. All the cars had smooth exteriors with flush-fitting windows and the sides swept down into a flare at car-floor level. The sliding air-worked doors were under the control of the guard. No one could now jump on to the running board of a moving train and struggle to pull the hand-operated door open before the train went into the tunnel. The clerestory roofs of much of the older stock gave way to smooth elliptical roofs in the new. Although three types of stock are mentioned, they really differed only in electrical equipment, and modifications to the 'O' and 'P' stock made the trailers so much alike that they were classified 'OP' and were virtually interchangeable. The 'Q' stock remained on the District until it was withdrawn in 1970.

After the war it was decided that the eastern end of the District Line should be modernized in conjunction with the electrification of the London, Tilbury & Southend tracks. The L.T. & S. lines, formerly steam-worked, were to be electrified at the industrial frequency and at 25,000V., a system quite different from London Transport's, and the simplest thing was to segregate the District and L.T. & S. lines – there were already four tracks, but it was necessary to remodel sidings, eliminate cross-overs, etc. and in particular to construct a flyover and dive-under at Barking to give cross-platform interchange between London Transport and Eastern Region trains proceeding in the same direction. The London Transport tracks were completely resignalled to London Transport standards, and a new rolling stock depot was built at Upminster. At Plaistow the old sub-station was replaced by a new one equipped to modern standards. Special precautions were taken with the signalling to ensure that no interference with circuits was caused by the high-voltage overhead equipment on the Eastern Region lines alongside. An important effect of the segregation of the running lines was to improve running and cut out delays at the eastern end of the District Line which had reactions right back to the western end of the line.

The postponed Metropolitan Line scheme was re-examined, and it was decided in 1956 to proceed with the works. Some of these had to be re-planned, and there were slight changes from the original ideas, but the plan which emerged again provided for four tracks north of Harrow-on-the-Hill and for extending electrification from Rickmansworth to Amersham and Chesham. When the works were finished it was expected that more and faster trains could be run. Amersham, 23.9 miles from Baker Street Junction, was to be the new terminus of the Metropolitan Line, which was thus contracting still farther into its role of an urban and suburban railway after its venture into the country in Watkin's days. The stations north of Amersham – Great Missenden, Wendover, Stoke Mandeville, and Aylesbury – were to be served only by British Railways' trains, and the first three would join Aylesbury in British Railways' hands.

The Metropolitan electrification works were started in 1958 and completed in 1960. The first trial train reached Amersham under electric power on 15 August 1960, and the last steam passenger train on the Chesham branch ran on the night of 11/12 September. The shuttle trains on this branch were made up of coaches of 'Ashbury' stock and were probably among the oldest standard-gauge coaches then in regular service in Britain. Five of the six coaches concerned were marked for preservation, four of them as working stock on the Bluebell Railway.

On the same date, 12 September, the electrified lines to Amersham were brought into use for trains not proceeding farther, but Aylesbury trains continued to change to steam traction at Rickmansworth, using the existing locomotive-changing facilities. The last day of steam working on the Metropolitan, and indeed of passenger train steam working on London Transport lines as a whole, was duly celebrated on Saturday, 9 September 1961, and on the Monday the all-electric service started with no London Transport trains travelling beyond Amersham, which became the new terminus on that day. (The service had been all-electric on Sundays for some time, and Amersham had been the Sunday terminus.) From that day Chesham, 25.7 miles from Baker Street Junction, has been the most distant outpost of the Metropolitan – as indeed it was for a short while many years before. The modernization work was finished, and a completely new pattern of train service introduced, on 18 June 1962. New trains were being rapidly brought into use for the service by London Transport, and British Railways were bringing in modern multiple-unit diesel trains for their outer-suburban type of service.

The main purpose behind the Metropolitan Line programme was to increase the service where it was most required because of housing developments and the growing dormitory population – a cause of worry, as we have seen, even before the war. After the war, with people living farther out in the country, it was the area between Rickmansworth, Amersham, and Chesham which particularly needed an improved service, and the plans were to give three types of service – fast, semi-fast, and local – with overlapping where necessary to ensure good connections between the three types of trains. The British Railways diesel trains would be carrying the longest-distance traffic, and they were therefore given a fast run by letting them travel non-stop between Chorleywood and Harrow. One feature of the generally faster services of all types was that trains ran to a 'clock-face' pattern, with departures at regular intervals and at a fixed number of minutes past the hour.

The engineering works entailed a completely new station at Moor Park, an extensively rebuilt station at Northwood, and major additions to Amersham station. New substations were built at Chalfont and Chorleywood to supply the newly electrified track, and the extensive signalling work included a new signal cabin of unusual design at Amersham. Rolling-stock sidings were built at Rickmansworth and a new bay platform at Chesham. The modernization work involved alterations to 29 bridges, of which 17 were rebuilt or widened to take extra tracks. The largest new bridge was a 160 ft. long skew structure near Northwood. At several stations platforms had to be lengthened to take the new Metropolitan trains and the even longer diesels of British Railways.

As well as the compartment steam trains it was desired to get rid of the electric compartment stock, which was old and required replacement if an efficient and trouble-free service were to be given. To replace this older stock London Transport ordered 248 cars of a modern lightweight type constructed largely of aluminium alloy and left unpainted. This, the 'A' stock, is of the open saloon type with a centre gangway, has automatic doors under the control of the guard, and has the necessary capacity to cope with the heavy in-town peak traffic. It has fewer seats than the stock it replaced, but it met the Ministry of Transport requirements for cars used in single-line tunnels, which the old stock did not. The seating capacity is made up by the more frequent services and the fact that in the peak all trains are of eight cars. Twenty-seven similar trains were ordered for the Uxbridge branch. With the end of the compartment stock, all London Transport trains were of open saloon type with power-operated doors.

Comparatively few new tube cars were ordered during the immediate post-war years, though there were 92 new cars of the 1949 stock (as opposed to conversions), which resembled the 1938 stock in most ways but had simplified driving equipment built in at one end. This was to allow the three-car set of a seven-car train to be driven into the sidings independently when trains were uncoupled in off-peak hours. As well as 70 cars bought from the Birmingham Railway Carriage & Wagon Co. Ltd., 22 of these cars were built from converted 1938 stock which had been used in an unsuccessful experiment in running nine-car trains on the Northern Line, with end cars stopping at the platforms at selected stations only. Eighteen more trailers were produced from experimental streamlined tube stock which had spent the war in store at Cockfosters depot, and 21 trailers were purchased from the Birmingham Railway Carriage & Wagon Co. Ltd. In 1957–58, however, London Transport brought into service on the Piccadilly Line three prototype trains of a new type. In many ways their arrangement from the passenger's point of view resembled the 1938 stock, but they had fluorescent lighting and were 'all-silver', being clad in unpainted aluminium alloy panels. Below the skin there were further differences: bogies and axleboxes with rubber suspension, door-fault indicator lights, and a new roller-blind destination indicator at high-level on the front of the train where it would not be masked by people standing on station platforms – features also of the Metropolitan 'A' stock. Inside they also had a better arrangement of transverse seats so that passengers could move in and out more easily. Not long after the third of these trains, each from a different manufacturer, had been delivered, London Transport ordered 532 cars of this stock (1959 tube stock) from Metropolitan-Cammell.

For the Central Line, which in general had the oldest stock, a new type of train was designed, and twelve motor cars of a completely new pattern were purchased from Cravens Limited. They were also finished in unpainted aluminium alloy and had rubber bogie and axlebox suspension, but the bodies had a pronounced tumblehome to the sides above the waist and the front of the driving cab also sloped back. Windows were double-width, and great attention was paid to reducing noise, including the provision of perforated panels for the ceilings. These 12 motor cars ran with 12 trailers converted from the older tube stock and painted silver.

Unfortunately it was impossible to test these cars sufficiently before the imminence of the Eastern Region electrification from Liverpool Street to Chingford, Enfield Town, Bishop's Stortford, and Hertford East made it essential to have new stock ready for the expected influx of traffic to the Central Line at Liverpool Street. A further 676 cars of the 1959 stock were therefore ordered and deliveries were switched to the Central Line while the Piccadilly was still short of 57 new trains. When the Central Line (except for its shuttle services) had been equipped with new trains, deliveries to the Piccadilly Line were resumed.

The District also had some post-war stock to replace the outworn 'C', 'D', and 'E' classes. This was the 'R' stock, which looked very much like the 'Q' stock but differed from it electrically, particularly in the fact that all 'R' stock cars were motored. Some of the 'R' stock was converted from 'Q' stock trailers, which were designed with conversion in mind. These converted cars formed the 'R38' stock. The 'R47' stock was made up of 143 cars built by the Birmingham Railway Carriage & Wagon Co. Ltd. (89 cars) and the Gloucester Railway Carriage & Wagon Co. Ltd. (54 cars).

The 'R49' cars were the first aluminium-alloy cars of light-weight integral construction to be built in quantity in Britain. These 90 cars arrived in 1952/53 and were nearly six tons lighter than similar vehicles in steel, with consequent saving in current consumption. These cars were built by the Metropolitan-Cammell Carriage & Wagon Co. Ltd.

One eight-car train was left unpainted. Twenty further 'R' stock cars went into service in 1959. Thirteen of these were new cars by Metro-Cammell; the other seven were converted from 'Q38' trailers and painted silver to run with the 13 unpainted aluminium cars.

The foundations of modern Underground rolling stock design were laid by W. A. Agnew, who came to the Metropolitan District Railway from Scotland as Rolling Stock Superintendent in 1904 specifically for the electrification of the system. He subsequently became Mechanical Engineer for all Underground Group lines and the first Chief Mechanical Engineer of the LPTB.

Probably no single man has had more influence on the design of London Transport's recent rolling stock than his successor W. S. Graff-Baker. Born an American, educated in Britain, and subsequently naturalized, he joined the Metropolitan District Railway as a junior fitter at the age of 20 and rose to be Chief Mechanical Engineer (Railways) in 1935. From then until his death in 1952 he was responsible for the design of rolling stock which long remained modern in appearance and some of which is still in daily service. He was also responsible for the lightweight aluminium alloy District Line stock, the first aluminium alloy stock to be used in quantity in Great Britain.

Graff-Baker was succeeded by A. W. Manser, who was responsible for the design of the 'silver' trains which have replaced much of the older stock on both sub-surface and deep tube lines. He in turn was succeeded by G. S. Bingham, the last Chief Mechanical Engineer (Railways). The Chief Mechanical Engineer is now responsible for both rail and road vehicles.

XV Expansion Again: The Victoria Line

EVEN WHILE the war was still in progress, a County of London Plan was being prepared by J. H. Forshaw, architect to the London County Council, and Professor Sir Patrick Abercrombie. This appeared in 1943. The planners were somewhat concerned that their ideas for the layout of the new London were often frustrated by the presence of railway embankments and viaducts, or railway frontages, yards, and sidings. They wanted to get these railway works under the ground as much as possible, but at the same time they recognized the importance of the railways in the movement of the people and freight of the area. Briefly, the plan proposed the placing underground of some of the main London railway termini and the resiting of others, the separation of main line and suburban traffic at the railway termini, and full-scale tube railways to take main-line stock and give underground connections between various main line stations. Where possible the new large tubes were to connect with the existing London Transport tube system. The northern half of the Inner Circle was to be used as a freight route.

The planners themselves realized that there was a great difference between what was desirable and what was practicable with a great transport system on which millions of people depended and which would have to be kept going during any changes. They suggested the formation of a special investigating committee, and in due course the Railway (London Plan) Committee was appointed by the Minister of War Transport. The chairman was Professor Sir Charles Inglis and the membership included the Ministry's chief inspecting officer of railways and several prominent railwaymen. The committee found itself unable to agree with the earlier planners on many points and put forward suggestions of its own which would have entailed, among other things, a number of new tube lines.

A further body, called the 'Working Party', was set up to consider the effects of the scheme proposed by the Railway (London Plan) Committee and the extent to which they met the long-term requirements of passenger traffic.

The new body was concerned with traffic requirements as known after the war, and it was to be expected that its proposals would have a more practical ring about them. In broad principle, it stated that outer suburban areas should have fast or semi-fast train services with main-line size trains and a high number of seats. Urban services, up to a maximum of 12–14 miles from the centre, should be provided by stopping trains of tube size, with a fair number of seats but a capacity for heavy overload and provision for large numbers of passengers to enter or leave trains at stations. It agreed that the outer suburban trains could cross London in 17 ft. diameter tubes and thus enable one of the railway bridges across the Thames (Blackfriars) to be removed – bridge removal being a particular requirement of the town planners. Other recommendations of the Working Party were that the all-stations services should run on self-contained tracks and not be interworked with semi-fast or freight trains, and that no more than three tube lines should intersect at any station.

The two main tube lines recommended by the Working Party (apart from the main-line tubes, which are more expensive to build) were what they called Routes C and D. Route C was a north-south line starting in the Tottenham/Edmonton area and running via Finsbury Park, King's Cross, Euston, Oxford Circus, Green Park, Victoria, Vauxhall, Stockwell, Brixton, and Streatham to East Croydon, with possible branch lines at the northern end on the alignment of the Cambridge Road and from Seven Sisters to Walthamstow. Route D assumed the electrification of the Eastern Region services to Chingford and Enfield Town. The new tube would be connected to these suburban lines at Hackney Downs and then run via Liverpool Street, Bank, Ludgate Circus, Aldwych, and Trafalgar Square to Victoria. At a later date (lower priority) this line might continue via Knightsbridge, Kensington High Street, and Olympia and then along the line of the Uxbridge Road to Yeading Lane.

As the high cost of the work made it unlikely that more than one new tube railway could be built at one time, it was decided that the work of detailed planning should be concentrated on the line which would bring the quickest general benefit to London. That line was Route C. It was given preference over Route D because it would give a badly-needed tube facility to the suburbs – all densely populated – of Tottenham, Edmonton, and Walthamstow. It would also relieve the most heavily loaded of all the sections of London Transport's tube lines – the Piccadilly Line, especially between King's Cross and Finsbury Park. (See the map on page 150.)

Equally important, there were other benefits to be derived from Route C in inner London. It would connect King's Cross and Euston in the north with Oxford Circus and Green Park, and with the Westminster business area. From the other direction it would give passengers arriving by Southern Region trains at Victoria a direct route to Oxford Street, the West End, and the Euston Road area with its mainline stations. It would open up alternative routes which would ease congestion all over the central section of the Underground and save time on many journeys by giving quicker ways of getting from one place to another.

The original proposal showed possible branches up the Lea Valley or to Walthamstow. On balance, the second of these destinations seemed to have the higher priority. The line would therefore start from Wood Street on the Chingford Line, which was itself proposed to become part of Route D. It would then run across the Lea Valley to Seven Sisters and then under Seven Sisters Road to Manor House. The first idea was that Route C should use the existing Piccadilly Line Manor House station, the Piccadilly being diverted into new through tunnels to give a non-stop run from Finsbury Park to Turnpike Lane. (This proposal was later dropped). At the next station, Finsbury Park, use was to be made of the existing Northern City Line station tunnels, as it was expected that by then the Northern City trains would have been diverted from these tunnels to the unfinished surface station alongside the Eastern Region trains and thence over newly electrified Eastern Region tracks to East Finchley and Alexandra Palace. With some re-arrangement of the use of these tunnels and those of the Piccadilly Line alongside, same-level interchange could be provided between Route C and the Piccadilly Line.

From Finsbury Park it was intended that Route C should run direct to King's Cross with no intermediate stations. As it looked as though Route D would be some way in the future, however, it was decided to divert Route C a little to the east and give same-level interchange with the Northern City line at Highbury. This would give a convenient route to Moorgate and the City for Route C passengers.

At King's Cross the Working Party's limit of three tube lines intersecting at one station was to be reached. At this station neither the Piccadilly nor the Northern Lines ran in a direction which would enable the new line to come in alongside and give same-level interchange. The ground-space under King's Cross is very crowded and the only place for Route C was above the Piccadilly Line and under the Circle Line, which is just below the surface. At the lowest level of all is the Northern Line. On the surface, of course, is the Eastern Region's King's Cross terminus with St. Pancras on the other side of Pancras Road. As well as the access shafts and interchange subways connected with the tube and Circle Lines, there are tunnels leading from the Widened Lines to the London Midland Region and Eastern Region tracks. There are also the Fleet sewer, public lavatories, and pedestrian subways under Pancras and Euston Roads.

At Euston same-level interchange was to be provided with the City loop of the Northern Line. This entailed right-hand running for Route C at Euston, to be achieved by 'rolling' the two tubes over each other between Highbury and King's Cross and back again between Warren Street and Oxford Circus. The main object of this interchange would be to encourage passengers from the northern suburbs to use City Line trains when they were travelling to the West End and change at Euston, as well as using the through trains via Charing Cross. This would even up the loading and number of trains on the two Northern Line routes and enable a more balanced service to be given. The more convenient Euston interchange would also give some relief to the heavily-used interchange stations at Tottenham Court Road, Leicester Square, and Charing Cross.

The next station, Warren Street, also was not in the original scheme but was added for several reasons. It would give an interchange with the Charing Cross side of the Northern Line; it would give a new facility at a busy intersection – Tottenham Court Road and Hampstead Road with Euston Road; and it would break into a long section of line between Euston and Oxford Circus, which it was felt was too far (over a mile) without a station in central London. Another reason was that it might be possible to build a new station on the Circle Line at this point, with inter-connecting subways, as part of a rationalization scheme for the stations along the Euston Road/Marylebone Road alignment.

At Oxford Circus it was apparent that the already hard-pressed station facilities, dealing with only two lines (Central and Bakerloo), would have to be extensively improved to deal with the traffic, including interchange traffic, for three lines. A virtually new station was planned, with a new booking hall under the Circus itself and escalators to all lines, and with same-level interchange between the Bakerloo Line and Route C.

The next station was Green Park, where heavy interchange traffic was expected. As the Piccadilly Line and the new line would cross almost at right-angles, however, it was impossible to provide same-level interchange.

The next station, Victoria, would be a combined Route C and Route D tube station, with interchange between the two lines over the platforms and a separate interchange at an intermediate level with the District and Circle Line station.

After consideration it was decided that the Lea Valley crossing in the north should be by tube all the way; this would enable the stations to be sited in the best possible places from the traffic point of view. The final section of the line, however, would rise to the surface to give interchange with the Eastern Region Line at Wood Street. A depot, reached by a tube connection, would be provided in the Northumberland Park area.

Here then was a new route reduced to a real possibility – the first new tube route across central London since 1907, when the Charing Cross route of the Northern Line was built. There was no doubt that it was needed. Traffic was growing as London spread, and by 1954 passengers arriving at Victoria (Southern Region) had increased by 40 per cent over the pre-war figures. In a talk to the Institute of Transport on 5 December 1955, Sir John Elliot, who had become Chairman of London Transport on 1 October 1953 on the retirement of Lord Latham, suggested the name 'Victoria Line' for Route C, and the Victoria Line it has been ever since. On the same occasion he made an eloquent statement of the social benefits of the line to London in saving of time and relief of traffic congestion (by diversion of car owners to the much quicker Victoria Line instead of their own cars). He also stated that the British Transport Commission Bill which would give the necessary Parliamentary powers to build the new line was even then awaiting its third reading in the House of Lords and was nearly on the Statute Book. Prophetically, he said: 'finance is the stumbling block which might prevent the building of the new tube'.

Support for the new line came from many directions. A Political & Economic Planning broadsheet of 1956 claimed that underground railways were a much better investment than urban motorways in areas of high land value like central London, and that the advantage to be gained in carrying passengers was so great that a strong case could be made for the cost being met from public funds. The London Transport Annual Review for 1956 explained that powers to build the line had been obtained in the British Transport Commission Act, 1955, but that work could not be put in hand until the means of financing the expenditure had been settled and that that question was still under consideration between London Transport, the B.T.C., and the Government. Technical planning, however, was going ahead.

By 1959 the money was still not forthcoming, but by now the preparation of detailed surveys and plans was well advanced and boreholes had been sunk along the length of the line between Walthamstow and Victoria – for that was as far as the line would go at first. Powers were being sought in Parliament to make further alterations to the Northern City tunnels at Highbury to give same-level interchange with the Victoria Line. Schemes for nine of the thirteen stations had been approved, and contract drawings were being prepared by the consulting engineers, Sir William Halcrow & Partners and Messrs. Mott, Hay & Anderson. Negotiations were in progress with British Railways on the detailed design of the sub-surface stations at Euston and King's Cross.

In the same year, it was decided to test new methods of tunnelling and tunnel lining which, if successful, would enable the Victoria Line to be built more cheaply. Orders were placed for cast-iron and concrete types of lining and for shields, and contracts for tunnelling were let to Kinnear Moodie & Co. Ltd. and Edmund Nuttall, Sons & Co. Ltd. They were to start at Finsbury Park and a site on the corner of Netherton Road and Seven Sisters Road, and tunnel towards each other under the line of Seven Sisters Road, and under the park at Finsbury Park. Half the tunnels – there were to be twin tubes – would be lined with concrete segments and half with a flexible-jointed cast-iron lining without bolts and with much shallower flanges than were usual in the standard type of lining. The contractors were to join up near Manor House station on the Piccadilly Line. Using a new rotary type of shield called a 'drum digger', these tunnels were built in record time. Using the cast-iron lining, Edmund Nuttall, Sons & Co. Ltd. built 934 ft. of tunnel in two weeks, or 3 ft. of tube tunnel, including lining, per working hour. This was believed to be a world record for driving and lining a tunnel of this size (12 ft. 8 in. internal diameter) in clay soil and was double the speed which could be expected with previous techniques. On completion, one of the mile-long tunnels was extended to join the southbound Northern City platform at Finsbury Park. It was then possible to lay rails in the new tunnel and run a train into it when required for a full-scale programme of testing to see how the new forms of lining behaved in various circumstances, including the simulated sinking of deep foundations, as for a tall building, close to the tunnels. The experimental tunnelling was under the control of London Transport's chief civil engineer, C. E. Dunton.

While all this was going on, other improvements were being carried out on the existing system. New signalling techniques with 'programme machines' for the automatic working of junctions* were being tried out; the Metropolitan Line programme was in full swing; arrangements were in hand to replace nearly half the rolling stock on the system by new trains; and a reconstruction scheme at Notting Hill Gate, which was combining the former Circle and Central Line stations and giving London its first sight of what a post-war Underground station should be, was nearly finished.

For the Victoria Line there had been a period in which detailed planning went ahead, but repeated questions in Parliament by interested Members were met with the reply that the line was still being considered. The times were not propitious.

On 28 April 1953 the Minister of Transport, the Rt. Hon. A. T. Lennox-Boyd, M.P., announced that a Committee of Inquiry (usually known now as the Chambers Committee after S. P. Chambers, its chairman) was to be set up 'to enquire into the conduct of the London Transport undertaking . . . and to report'. In its Report, which was published in 1955, the committee stated that the indirect advantages of Route C to London Transport and to London's economy as a whole were so important that 'this project should not be abandoned or postponed because on the basis of direct revenue or direct expenditure it appears to be unprofitable'.

A report on the Victoria Line by the London Travel Committee to the Minister of Transport and Civil Aviation, published in 1959, stated in its final paragraph; 'We recommend that the Victoria Line as it is at present planned should be authorized forthwith and construction put in hand as quickly as possible. . . . This decision has only been taken after the most exhaustive examination of all the many factors involved.'

At last, quite suddenly, Government approval was given for the Victoria Line on 20 August 1962.

*The operation of 'programme machines' is described briefly on page 132.

The line as authorized had been changed somewhat from Route C as originally planned. In the interim period the Eastern Region lines to Enfield Town and Chingford had been electrified on the high-voltage a.c. system, and consideration was being given to the electrification of the Great Northern suburban lines from King's Cross. This opened up the possibility of the Northern City line being used to take Eastern Region electric trains from Finsbury Park to Moorgate. (The scheme for running Northern City trains to Alexandra Palace had died completely when British Railways closed that line in 1956.)

The electrification of the Enfield and Chingford lines had also solved the problem of Route D as part of the British Railways Chingford branch. It had therefore been decided that money could be saved and an effective interchange with the Chingford line be given equally well by cutting back the Victoria Line to Walthamstow Hoe Street instead of Wood Street. This meant that the line would not come to the surface at all, the Victoria Line Hoe Street station being underground whereas the Wood Street station would have been on the surface.

Apart from this, the Victoria Line is very much Route C as planned so long before. A mile of it was already in being, as the experimental tunnels were built on the proposed alignment of the Victoria Line, and the rest of the work was to take 6½ years from the start – the time being dictated by the station works, especially Oxford Circus station, rather than the tunnelling. The main section of the line is 10½ miles long and has 12 stations, 11 of which give interchange with other Underground or British Railways lines. The average depth is 69 ft., and, unlike earlier tube lines, the Victoria Line does not follow the line of streets unless they already point in the right direction (as Seven Sisters Road does). It runs from Victoria via Green Park, Oxford Circus, Warren Street, Euston, King's Cross, Highbury, and Finsbury Park, as described, and then direct to Seven Sisters, where the new station has been built between Tottenham High Road and the Eastern Region station (Seven Sisters), with interchange escalators and stairs. The next station is Tottenham Hale, where the Victoria Line station adjoins that of the Eastern Region, with escalators to and from the Eastern Region Cambridge Line and to Ferry Lane. Next comes Blackhorse Road at the junction of Blackhorse Road and Forest Road and finally Walthamstow Central (formerly Walthamstow (Hoe Street)).

PLATE 47. New bridge at Chigwell carrying the Central Line over the route of the M.11 motorway

PLATE 48. Piccadilly Line train terminating at Hatton Cross before the line was opened through to Heathrow Central

PLATE 49. Building Heathrow Central Station. The deep concrete 'box' which contains the platforms, ticket hall, electrical substation, and escalators can be seen in the foreground

PLATE 50. Platform-level at Heathrow Central, with two trains waiting to depart for London

PLATE 51. Partly-completed cut-and-cover section of the Heathrow extension showing the intersecting Secant piling used for the side walls with the characteristic markings impressed on the piles by the withdrawal of the steel sleeves in which they are formed

PLATE 52. Interior of a new Piccadilly Line car showing splayed door screens, split-level armrests and high-level glazing in the doors to enable standing passengers to see station names

PLATE 53. Inaugural train on the Heathrow Extension of the Piccadilly Line about to break the tape, with the Queen in the cab.

PLATE 54. New rolling stock seen in 1974 on the Northern Line. These cars, which have painted doors, are running on the first stage of the Jubilee Line which opened in Spring 1979

Plate 55. Tunnelling work in progress on the Jubilee Line, showing a ring of bolted iron segments in course of erection. One of the mechanical diggers used on parts of the line can be seen in the foreground

Plate 56. One of the Jubilee Line trains passing through the new automatic washing-machines at Neasden depot

PLATE 57. Special shield, designed to use Bentonite slurry for working in loose ground, in experimental use near New Cross

PLATE 58. A view of part of Stonebridge Park Depot of the Bakerloo Line, nearing completion in Spring 1979

PLATE 59. 'Umbrella' decking being installed at Bond Street Station to allow the new station ticket hall to be built beneath the street while traffic continues normally

PLATE 60. New ticket office at Bond Street, modernized for the extra traffic expected with the opening of the Jubilee Line

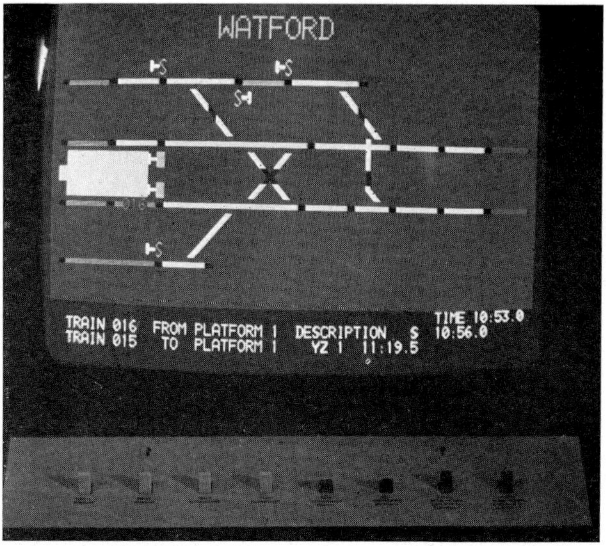

PLATE 61. Visual display unit in Rickmansworth signal cabin showing the state of computer-controlled points and signals at Watford. The display also shows where trains are standing in the station and sidings

PLATE 62. Three-language journey-planner showing on a television-type screen, the route between any-two stations

The depot is in the open at Northumberland Park and is reached via a junction in tunnel near Seven Sisters station and then by tunnel to the surface.

The effects in reducing congestion on other lines are proving to be as predicted a decade before, with special benefit to the Piccadilly Line between Manor House and Holborn, and to a lesser but important degree on the District Line between Charing Cross and Victoria. The Central Line also benefits because some passengers from the Woodford area and others from Walthamstow who formerly travelled by bus to Leyton, or travelled by Eastern Region services to change to it at Liverpool Street, now use the Victoria Line. The Northern Line is helped between Tottenham Court Road and Charing Cross by the new direct Victoria–Oxford Circus link.

The first work on the Victoria Line after authorization began on 20 September 1962 when pneumatic drills broke the surface of Oxford Circus at the start of exploratory work to determine the sites for supports for an 'umbrella' bridge to carry road traffic over the Circus while the new station was built beneath. Oxford Circus was the first job to be started and among the last to be finished.

There followed the letting of a series of contracts which was eventually to embrace tunnel lining segments in cast iron and concrete, mechanical excavator and Greathead type shields, civil engineering works, building and finishing works, the rolling stock depot at Northumberland Park, sleepers, new automatically-driven trains, special signalling equipment, automatic fare collection equipment, and all the other things which made up London's new Underground railway.

By the end of 1963, contracts worth £22 million had already been placed. A substantial amount of work had been done at the Victoria, Oxford Circus, Euston, Highbury, and Seven Sisters station sites, as well as on the Northern Line diversion works at Euston and the similar Northern City Line diversion at Highbury. Over 30 working sites were in use and more than 20 working shafts had been sunk. In the same year, specifications for the trains were brought to the point where tenders could be invited.

In 1963 work began on the modernization of Lots Road generating station, which was to be converted from $33\frac{1}{3}$ cycle operation to 50 cycles and have its coal-burning equipment replaced by six new oil-fired boilers of advanced type feeding six 30,000 kW turbo-alternators. A major modernization of the distribution network, including new switchhouses and new and improved substations, was also being undertaken. The scheme included the provision of power supplies to the Victoria Line. Among other things, the power supply programme was to result in the closing of Neasden generating station and the linking of Lots Road and Greenwich (the former tramway generating station) by 22,000V. cables to permit exchange of power in an emergency and more efficient operation generally. Lots Road was to lose two of its 275 ft. chimneys, which the new boilers would not need.

In April 1964, following preliminary tests on the District Line, four four-car trains fitted with automatic driving equipment, using a system devised by London Transport's engineers, were placed in service on the Hainault–Woodford section of the Central Line for extended trials to prove the practicability of this type of operation. The success of the trials led to the adoption of automatic driving for the Victoria Line, with consequent saving in manpower and electric current, and more regular and uniform running of the trains. With this system, the one-man crew – the train operator – opens and closes the doors at a station and then presses twin 'start' buttons which bring the automatic mechanism into operation. The train starts and accelerates, coasts and brakes, obeying coded commands from the track, until it comes to a stop at the next station. An independent safety signalling system ensures that the trains are stopped if there is a train on the next section of track or if anything should go wrong with the automatic driving equipment. The train operator, who is in the cab at the front of the train, can take charge and drive manually at slow speed if needed.

The order for the bodies and bogies of the Victoria Line trains – 244 cars in all – was placed with the Metropolitan-Cammell Carriage & Wagon Co. Ltd. They were to be of eight cars in two four-car units, each with two motor and two trailer cars. The odd four-car unit was for replacement purposes while other units were out of service for maintenance and overhaul.

The first trial installations of automatic fare collection equipment, with three different types of automatic ticket gate at three District Line stations – Stamford Brook, Chiswick Park, and Ravenscourt Park – also came in 1964. The principle, which remained the same in the full-scale trial equipment installed on the Victoria Line, is that a ticket is magnetically encoded at the time of issue with various particulars, including the date, the fare paid, and the station at which it was issued. At the beginning of a journey, the ticket is inserted into an automatic gate which 'reads' the coded information and, if the ticket is valid, returns it to the passenger and frees or opens the gate to let him pass through to the platform. At the end of the journey the ticket is inserted into another gate, which again 'reads' the coding, checks the details of the fare paid, date, station of issue, etc., against those in its memory store, and – if the ticket is valid – lets the passenger through so that he can leave the station. The gate retains the ticket in this case. These methods of selling and checking tickets give better control and are a deterrent to fraudulent travel.

Two types of gate were used for the Victoria Line, one a 'four-door' gate which opens one pair of doors to let the passenger step into a space with another pair of doors ahead. As the passenger steps through the first pair of doors, the second pair opens in front of him and the first pair closes behind. The other type was a three-armed turnstile gate, in which valid tickets release the turnstile so that one passenger at a time can step through. Both types of gate were capable of being reversed and used for business-bound passengers in the morning and homeward-bound passengers at night.

A new development with the four-door gate was first tried at Seven Sisters in November 1970. Instead of being normally closed and opened only when a ticket is inserted, the gates were left open. Provided a valid ticket is inserted, the gates remain open for a passenger to walk through. If no ticket is inserted, or an incorrect ticket, the gates close to bar the way. The reason is that gates need overhaul after about a million operations – a figure reached in nine months or so at busy stations. If this system were successful – and the trials were extended to Green Park station also in October 1971 – the reduced number of operations would cut down wear and tear so that overhauls would be years instead of months apart. However, an important change in policy came in 1972 in regard to automatic fare collection (see page 148).

On 5 October 1964 trains were withdrawn from the Finsbury Park–Drayton Park section of the Northern City Line to allow work to be carried out on the station tunnels and part of the running tunnels at Finsbury Park, where the platform arrangements were being modified to let Piccadilly and Victoria Line trains run in on adjacent platforms for easy interchange.

A substitute coach service was introduced between Drayton Park and Finsbury Park and this continued to run until the opening of the first section of the Victoria Line (Walthamstow Central–Highbury) on 1 September 1968, re-opened a rail link, via the cross-platform interchange at Highbury, between Finsbury Park and the Northern City. The direct Drayton Park – Finsbury Park link by Underground has not been restored because the Eastern Region of British Railways has now electrified its King's Cross suburban routes, and has built a new connection between Finsbury Park high-level (British Railways) station and Drayton Park to allow suburban trains to run to Moorgate via the former Northern City Line (later known as the Highbury Branch of the Northern Line).

In 1965 the last three civil engineering contracts for the Victoria Line were let and by the end of the year more than half the station tunnels and three-quarters of the running tunnels had been completed, as well as many other works. C. E. Dunton, the Chief Civil Engineer, retired and was succeeded in October 1965 by H. G. Follenfant, who had had a good deal of responsibility for the earlier stages of the Victoria Line work and had been Deputy Chief Civil Engineer since 1964.

By the end of 1966 all the running tunnel shield drives and 23 of the 24 station tunnels had been completed, sleepers had been installed along 10 miles of running tunnel and four miles of long-welded rail were already in place. The Oxford Circus 'umbrella', installed during the August holiday weekend of 1963, was extended – again during the August holiday – to allow further work to be done under its protection.

In 1967, the first four-car unit of the Victoria Line stock arrived for tests to be followed by operation on the Woodford–Hainault line – to which all the new stock was to go in turn for tests in public service before being sent to the new depot at Northumberland Park, nearly completed by the end of the year. These trains had other new features as well as the automatic driving equipment. There were double-width, double-glazed windows all along the train and 'wrap-round' windows for the cabs. Door glazing was carried up higher to let standing passengers see station names without stooping. All seats in the trailer cars were arranged to face inwards, giving more standing space. Behind the scenes there was rheostatic braking for speeds down to about 10 m.p.h. as well as the normal braking systems used elsewhere on the Underground. The trains continued the use of unpainted aluminium alloy to give the 'silver' look characteristic of modern Underground stock. Their communication equipment included public address loudspeakers in all cars, inter-train radio links, and a special carrier-wave communication system which allowed the operator to speak to the Cobourg Street control centre at Euston, and vice versa, at any time, whether the train was moving or not.

The Victoria Line civil engineering work was virtually completed in 1967 and the finishing of stations was well in hand, as was the installation of all the equipment and cables needed in the tunnels, at stations, and elsewhere.

An important decision came in August 1967 when the Minister of Transport (Mrs. Barbara Castle) authorized the Victoria Line to be extended 3½ miles to Brixton, with intermediate stations at Vauxhall and Stockwell. The extension, Parliamentary powers for which were granted in 1966, was expected to relieve road and rail bottlenecks at the existing Thames crossing points, and to take some peak-hour traffic from sections of the heavily-loaded Bakerloo and Northern lines. Same-level interchange with the Northern Line was to be provided at Stockwell and interchange with the Southern Region at Vauxhall; Brixton was expected to prove a good interchange point for passengers arriving by bus or car. An additional station at Pimlico was under discussion during 1967 and the Minister approved the start of work on it during 1968. A further 72 cars were ordered to meet the additional rolling stock requirements of the extended line.

The social desirability of the extension was the subject of 'social benefit' studies, using a new, but already well-established, technique of balancing social costs against social benefits. This technique, of great potential importance to public undertakings, was pioneered by C. D. Foster and M. E. Beesley in their earlier study of the Victoria Line. The effect of these studies has been to demonstrate the impact of the new Underground lines on the community as a whole.

In 1968 everything came to a head. The Oxford Circus 'umbrella', by then almost a landmark in its own right, was removed during the Easter weekend. Finishing work reached a climax, the closed-circuit television system, with its 74 cameras and 42 monitor sets, was installed, and special tile motifs appeared on the platform walls of the new stations.

The television system is used in several ways. Cameras are mounted at each end of the platforms and at strategic points elsewhere in the stations, such as busy interchange concourses and at the foot of escalators. Most stations have an 'operations room' with monitor screens on which the pictures transmitted from any of the station's cameras can be viewed. Pictures from any of the platforms on the line can be viewed on screens at the Cobourg Street control centre. This visual information was expected to be – and is – of considerable use in dealing with crowd control, etc., on the line, and was tried experimentally for some years at Holborn station before the decision was made to equip the Victoria Line. It was decided to extend the closed-circuit television system to those parts of the stations which serve other lines, thus enabling the entire station to be observed from one central point and assisting in crowd control. The stations selected were Victoria, Green Park, Oxford Circus, Warren Street, Euston, and King's Cross.

There is also a television screen at the front end of each platform, facing the train. This screen shows the picture transmitted by the camera at the rear end of the platform and is provided to help the train operator, who can see, either directly or on the screen, what is happening all the way along the platform. Without the screen, his view could be obstructed by passengers and he would have difficulty in deciding when to close the train doors.

On Monday, 5 August 1968, the Chief Civil Engineer handed over the first section of the line – from Walthamstow Central to Highbury & Islington, to F. G. Maxwell, the Operating Manager (Railways), for training and test purposes.

On Sunday, 1 September, without special ceremony, the Walthamstow–Highbury section opened for public traffic, to be followed three months later, on Sunday, 1 December, by the Highbury–Warren Street section. On 2 January 1969 a Buckingham Palace announcement stated that the third stage – from Warren Street to Victoria – would be opened by Her Majesty the Queen on Friday, 7 March, bringing the Victoria Line, the most highly-automated Underground line in the world, into full commission.*

At 11 00 on 7 March the Queen arrived by car at Green Park station, bought a ticket from a machine, passed through the automatic gates and down the new flight of escalators to the platforms. There, recalling that in 1890 her great-grandfather, Edward VII, when Prince of Wales, had opened London's first electric Tube railway, she declared the new Victoria Line open. Then she entered a waiting train and moved into the cab, where she pressed the twin starting buttons to allow the train to move off through the new tunnels to Oxford Circus.

At Oxford Circus the Queen met many who had helped to turn the

Victoria Line from plan to reality – she had already met some at Green Park and was to meet others at Victoria – inspected the station, was shown how tickets are issued, and returned down the escalators to travel, this time as a passenger, to Victoria, where she unveiled a plaque in the ticket hall to commemorate the occasion.

A year after the line was opened it was carrying more than 1¼ million passengers a week.

* A full description of the Victoria Line is given in 'The Story of the Victoria Line', also published by London Transport.

XVI Into the New Age

ALTHOUGH THE Victoria Line was the focus of attention from 1962 onwards, other improvements to the Underground were still being carried out, some of a minor nature but some on a fairly large scale. At King's Cross, for example, the disused Metropolitan Line bay platform was converted to a wide new passenger concourse and brought into use in 1963. In the same year the construction of a new Tower Hill station, on the east side of Trinity Square and nearer to British Railways Fenchurch Street terminus, was authorized: the site was that of the short-lived Metropolitan station of 1882–4. The new station, which has a third platform for reversing trains, was opened and the old one closed on 5 February 1967.

Work began in 1963 on the realignment of the four tracks – two used by Metropolitan and Circle trains and the other two by trains of British Railways – between Moorgate and Aldersgate. This was to facilitate the carrying out of the City Corporation's Barbican scheme. The new tracks came into use in 1965. A by-product of the Barbican scheme was the renaming of Aldersgate station, which became Barbican on 1 December 1968.

In 1963, also, a series of commemorative events was held in celebration of the centenary of the Underground, including a parade of historic and modern rolling stock at Neasden. Appropriately, this look at the past was followed later in the year by the opening of a well-equipped training centre for future (and present) Underground railwaymen at White City.

The same year saw the return of London Transport to the status of a Board. Under the Transport Act, 1962, the British Transport Commission, in which London Transport had been vested under the Transport Act of 1947, was abolished and its properties and all its activities were distributed to four Boards – of which the London Transport Board was one – and the Transport Holding Company. The main effect as far as London Transport was concerned was to give it direct access and responsibility to the Minister of Transport, to whom major financial proposals had to be submitted for approval and from whom all long-term finance had to be borrowed.

This change was to be the beginning of a chain of events. Traffic congestion, the use of private cars, and the concentration of peak hour traffic into an even shorter period had reached such a pitch in 1964 that the London Transport Board thought it necessary to draw the Minister's attention to the fact that the mounting difficulties of running public transport made it doubtful whether the Board could both provide an adequate service of public transport *and* pay its way – two main duties prescribed by Parliament which were becoming increasingly difficult to reconcile. After considerable discussion, the Minister announced in June 1965 that the Board had been asked to postpone the fares increase needed to get its finances back into some semblance of balance until a thorough examination could be made of the conditions under which the Board had to operate. In order that the Board's position should not be made worse while the examination was being carried out, he gave an assurance that it would not have to bear the loss caused by the postponement of the fares increase. (At the end of 1965, the Minister paid London Transport £3,850,000 as compensation for postponing the increase.)

Further discussions followed between the Minister, the Greater London Council, and the Board. It so happened that in the first half of 1965 it was the Board's turn to have its activities investigated by the House of Commons Select Committee on Nationalized Industries, which examines all the nationalized industries in rotation. The debate on the Committee's report in December 1965 was the occasion for the Minister to make an official statement on policy, which included an assurance that the Government considered public transport essential and would ensure that it was not only maintained but improved, and that means would be found to 'achieve a more equitable distribution of the burden of paying for London's transport in all its forms.' This was to have far-reaching consequences.

The 1962 Act called for co-operation between the London Transport and British Railways Boards, and there were set up a Passenger Transport Committee for London and two sub-committees – the Passenger Transport Coordination Committee for London and the Passenger Transport Planning Committee for London. This last joint body was associated with the official 'South East Study' published in 1964, the exhaustive London Traffic Survey undertaken jointly by the London County Council (and its successor, the Greater London Council) and the Ministry of Transport, and with various aspects of regional planning. Against this background a tentative Railway Plan for London was prepared by a working party of the committee which set out, among other proposals, projects for new Underground lines.

The plan produced in March 1965 included three new lines – the extension of the Aldwych branch of the Piccadilly Line to Waterloo, the extension of the Victoria Line to Brixton, and a new tube line, to be known as the Fleet Line, which would be linked to the existing Stanmore branch of the Bakerloo Line and then run via the Strand and Fleet Street to the Lewisham area in south-east London.

Parliamentary powers for the Aldwych–Waterloo link were granted in 1965, and for the Brixton extension in 1966. The Fleet Line, as a new concept, needed more detailed study before the stage of applying for Parliamentary powers could be reached. The objects behind the proposals for the line included the relief of the busy Bakerloo Line, in particular between Piccadilly Circus, Paddington, and Finchley Road; the relief of the Central Line, particularly between Holborn and Liverpool Street; and the relief of the District Line, with which it would run parallel for part of its route.

Apart from these projects put forward by the planners, yet another prospect was the extension of the Hounslow branch of the Piccadilly Line to Heathrow Airport, and the desirability – and practicability – of doing this were under consideration. In many ways 1965 was an important year for forward Underground planning (see map of the Fleet Line on page 157).

The advances in thinking achieved in 1965 were carried on in the next year. The Government and the Board agreed to undertake a joint review, calling in outside experts as needed, of the Board's financial needs and commercial policies, and of the operating and management problems they presented. Meanwhile, the Government took powers under the Transport Finances Act of 1966 to provide grants of up to £16 million to cover revenue deficits expected to be incurred by London Transport while this review was being carried out.

In July 1966 the Minister (Mrs. Barbara Castle) published a White Paper on Transport Policy. This stated, *inter alia*, that single authorities should be established for major conurbations and these authorities should be responsible for highways, traffic, and public transport – all linked with the planning of land use, and also that public transport would need financial help. When such help is needed, it stated, the first source should be the local community, but the Government proposed to take powers to give financial assistance for the construction or major improvement of public transport facilities forming part of comprehensive transport plans.

Following this, and after consideration of the many factors involved, including views put forward by the Board on the constitution of a new authority for the London area which would deal with all the items set out by the White Paper, the Minister announced in December 1967 that the Greater London Council was to become the statutory transport planning authority for London, with wide responsibilities and powers for major highway functions, traffic, and public passenger transport services. The London Transport undertaking would be vested in a newly-formed London Transport Executive whose members would be appointed by the Council. The Executive was to be responsible for the day-to-day management of the Underground and buses while the Council would be responsible for overall policy and financial control. The proposals were incorporated in the Transport (London) Act 1969 and became effective on 1 January 1970.

The Transport Act 1968, which received the Royal Assent on 25 October 1968, included the promised powers for the Government to make grants (known as 'infrastructure grants') for the provision of new public transport facilities, with a maximum of 75 per cent for major railway projects.

During 1966 the last tube cars to have special compartments for the main control equipment were withdrawn, so that for the first time all rolling stock on the Underground was of the underfloor-equipment type. Fifty-one of the 'special compartment' cars passed through Acton Works for rehabilitation and were then sent to the Isle of Wight for use on the Southern Region's newly electrified lines on the island.

In May 1968, orders were placed for 212 cars of new design for the Hammersmith & City and Circle Lines. This stock, which runs in six-car trains, is capable of being operated by one man, though operated by two men at present, and has provision for automatic train operation (ATO) equipment to be fitted. The cars, built by Metro-Cammell Ltd., have four double doors on each side to speed up entry and exit on the busy in-town services on which they are operating: they also have air suspension – the first London Transport Underground trains to be so fitted. The first train came into use in the autumn of 1970 and the others were brought into use as they became available. The arrival of these trains – known as the C.69 stock – released cars running on the two lines for transfer to the District Line. This, in turn, enabled older District Line cars to be withdrawn from service – the last of the 'Q' stock trains was withdrawn on 24 September 1970. Except for the Wimbledon–Edgware Road service, where there are platform length restrictions which enforce the use of six-car trains, all District Line trains were re-formed to give a standard length of seven cars instead of the six- and eight-car lengths used formerly.

Design work had reached an advanced stage on the type of car which it was envisaged could replace the older trains on some tube lines, but orders for 30 seven-car trains for the Northern Line were placed early in 1971 and the first entered service on 26 June 1972. Except for the fact that they were operated by a two-man crew instead of automatically driven, these trains closely resembled those of the Victoria Line. Orders for another 33 trains of similar type, built like the previous 30 by Metro-Cammel Ltd. of Birmingham, were placed in November 1971. They qualified for a 75 per cent infrastructure grant from the Government – the scope of such grants having been widened to include replacement rolling stock – and the Greater London Council agreed to pay the other 25 per cent.

As well as automatic driving and automatic fare collection, London Transport developed 'programme machines' for automatic control of points and signals (or signal codes) in accordance with the working timetable, the relevant part of which is encoded and fed into the machine to form the 'programme' from which it operates. The use of these machines has been steadily extended since the first were introduced (at Kennington) in 1958. The machines are under remote supervision, notably (for the Northern and Victoria Lines) from the Cobourg Street control room. There is another large control room for District and Piccadilly Line installations at Earl's Court.

Another use of automatic control is at station car parks, the provision of which has been greatly extended by London Transport during the last few years. They now have space for some 12,000 cars. The automatic system incorporates 'rising steps' which prevent a car entering a car park unless space is available (cars are automatically counted in and out so that the machine 'knows' when there are vacant spaces) and, once inside, prevent it from leaving until the proper charge has been paid. Payment was originally made by coin-in-the-slot, but a token system was introduced later which had considerable advantage for the user. They can be bought in quantity at a discount, taking the place of a season ticket, but they will operate the barriers at any London Transport car park where tokens are in use instead of being available at only one station. Furthermore, unlike the season ticket holder, the token user does not pay for any day on which he does not use his car. The season ticket, of course, continues to have its cost advantages over daily payment at car parks not fitted for token operation.

As well as the modernization of Lots Road generating station, mentioned previously, a great deal of work has been done on the modernization of the power supply system and its switch-houses and substations. The whole system has been changed from the $33\frac{1}{3}$ c/s system to the 50 c/s system as used for the national grid. The Neasden generating station was closed down, after 64 years of continuous operation, in July 1968. It has now been demolished but a power supply is still obtained through a switch-house at Neasden from the Central Electricity Generating Board.

The closing down of Neasden left London Transport with two generating stations – Lots Road, the modernization of which was substantially completed in 1968 – and Greenwich, the former L.C.C. tramway power station, also in need of modernization. The decision was taken in 1968 that Greenwich should in future be regarded largely as a peak-load station which would supplement the main base-load station at Lots Road at periods of peak demand. The steam plant was to be removed and replaced with a number of gas-turbine units which could be started up quickly and brought into operation as required. This work, costing some £5 million, was completed in 1972, the last steam plant being closed down in February of that year. A feature of the scheme was that the gas-turbine units, designed to run initially on oil fuel, could be converted to operate on natural gas should that fuel become demonstrably cheaper than oil in the future. Conversion to use both fuels was undertaken in 1974 but the advantages of natural gas became more and more apparent as the North Sea fields were developed and it was decided that gas should be the normal fuel and oil the standby. The conversion of both generating stations was completed in 1977 and they are both now capable of running on gas or oil as desired; but gas at present (1978) has advantages over oil and both are using gas. The two stations, between them, supply more than two-thirds of the electricity consumed by London Transport, the remainder being drawn from the national grid.

The British Railways Eastern Region local line, with its stations, between Campbell Road Junction (Bow) and Upminster (except for Barking and Upminster stations) passed into London Transport hands from 1 January 1969. This made no difference to the train working, which had been carried out by London Transport as agent for British Railways for many years, but meant that the stations would as soon as possible be converted to London Transport standards and manned by London Transport staff. The fast lines, with the train service on them, remained in Eastern Region hands. London Transport has also taken over certain Western Region facilities between Westbourne Park and Paddington used in connection with the Hammersmith & City trains.

Underground expansion remains the key to rapid and easy commuter transport in London, and there is no lack of plans for new lines, some of which have already been briefly mentioned. Apart from the 3½-mile Brixton extension of the Victoria Line, there were plans for four new lines or extensions which can shortly be considered in more detail.

As recorded on an earlier page, the Minister of Transport authorized the start of work on the 3½-mile Brixton extension of the Victoria Line in August 1967, and work was pressed ahead steadily and without fuss. The Minister's announcement had declared that the extension would cost £16 million and should be in operation by 1972, carrying around 18 million passengers in its first year. It was also the first Underground extension to attract the new infrastructure grants which the Minister had obtained powers from Parliament to award in suitable cases. This brought the situation in London – and elsewhere – much nearer to that in other countries, where grants of this type from the state or regional or local governments had long been accepted. The Government agreed to meet 75 per cent of the total cost of £21 million and the Greater London Council met the other 25 per cent of the cost of work carried out after the Council became responsible for overall policy and financial control of London Transport at the beginning of 1970.

Two of the stations on the extension were completely new – Vauxhall and Brixton – but the third, Stockwell, was already served by the Northern Line. This station was rebuilt and enlarged with same-level interchange between the two lines and an additional escalator. The fourth station, Pimlico, was, as already explained, authorized rather later than the extension as a whole, so the platform tunnels were built and completely finished first so that there would be no obstruction to trains using the line but not, for the time being, stopping at this station. There is interchange at Vauxhall, by subway and ramp, with the Southern Region station.

Like the main Victoria Line, the Brixton extension provides many 'short-cuts' for Underground travellers. From Brixton to Oxford Circus, for example, takes 12½ minutes: the time from Stockwell to Oxford Circus is 10 minutes instead of 19 – a saving especially important to passengers from the southern end of the Northern Line with their easy interchange with the Victoria Line at Stockwell.

The individual tile motifs which are a feature of the main Victoria Line stations are also found on the extension. Pimlico's is an abstract composition – a herald of what is to be seen in the nearby Tate Gallery. At Vauxhall, an impression of wrought ironwork recalls an association with bygone revels at the once-notorious Vauxhall Gardens and a swan at Stockwell puts a well-known local landmark on the Underground map. Brixton's motif is a rebus – a visual pun on the station name in which bricks are the main ingredient.

The extension was ready for full operation on 12 July 1971, and a full service was run from that date – but without passengers – to test everything under everyday working conditions. Then, on the morning of Friday, 23 July 1971, Princess Alexandra formally opened the new line, pressing the start buttons to set her train in motion for the trip from Brixton to Pimlico (where the station was not yet open for public use) and then returning to Brixton as a passenger. There she unveiled a commemorative tablet in the ticket hall. At 15 00 the same day the extension was opened for passenger traffic. Pimlico station was opened by the Lord Mayor of Westminster on 14 September 1972. The opening of the Brixton extension brought a surge of extra traffic to an already popular line.

There had been plans for some time to serve Heathrow Airport either by main-line railway spur from the Southern Region at Feltham or by an extension of the Piccadilly Line. The terminus of the Piccadilly Line at Hounslow West was only two miles from the airport boundary and a 3½-mile extension would take the line into the heart of the airport terminal complex. In May 1970 the Heathrow Link Steering Group set up by the Minister of Transport and the President of the Board of Trade to assess possible rail links pronounced its preference for the Underground line. Welcoming that decision, London Transport announced that all preparations had been made to start construction within three months of the authorization of the work, which could be completed in something like four years. The cost would be £14·9 million, or, adding on the cost of associated works such as subways and travolators to link the station with the passenger buildings at the airport itself, and also the capitalization of interest during the construction period, about £19 million. A station at Hatton Cross on the edge of the airport would serve many of the large number of people employed at Heathrow – expected to rise eventually to 60,000.

The scheme, for which Parliamentary powers had been obtained in 1967, was approved in July 1970 by the Greater London Council, which announced its willingness to bear 25 per cent of the cost provided that the Government made a 75 per cent infrastructure grant. On 6 November 1970 a Government announcement accepted that the Underground link to the Airport should be built: on the grounds that the extension ought to pay its way the Government did not think a grant would be appropriate. The extension, therefore, went ahead with the G.L.C. grant of 25 per cent of the cost, and the remainder being found by raising a loan. A subsequent change of heart by the Government in July 1972 resulted in a further 25 per cent grant towards the cost of the Heathrow extension, leaving London Transport to bear half the cost.

The link entailed building a new platform to the north of the existing ones at Hounslow West and continuing in 'cut-and-cover' construction, rising to the surface for about 600 yards to cross the River Crane alongside the Great South West Road (A30). A further section of cut-and-cover to Hatton Cross was to be followed by a $1\frac{1}{4}$-mile twin tube tunnel section under the airport itself to an underground station serving the main buildings (see map on page 156).

The train service, in peak hours, was planned to run every four minutes but be slightly less at other times, though never falling below one train every $7\frac{1}{2}$ minutes. Although many passengers were expected to join the Heathrow line from stations elsewhere on the Underground network and disperse from the airport in similar fashion, visitors to London would be able to reach Gloucester Road, at the centre of a large hotel area, in 30 minutes or continue to the West End, or go on to the Russell Square and Bloomsbury hotel area. Of 42,000 hotel beds in Central London, nearly two-thirds were calculated to be within half-a-mile of Piccadilly Line stations. Still more hotel development was in progress in areas served by the Piccadilly Line.

Many air passengers travel light with brief cases or only one suitcase and the Underground has always carried many travellers with luggage on their journeys between the main London railway termini, but the Piccadilly Line trains serving the airport were to have extra space by the doors where luggage could stand without causing obstruction.

The first contract for work on the Heathrow Airport link was let in March 1971 to W. & C. French (Construction) Ltd. for civil engineering work on the two-mile section between Hounslow West station and Hatton Cross. It was worth roundly £4 million and included the diversion of the Piccadilly Line at Hounslow, station works at Hounslow and Hatton Cross, and the construction of the bridge over the River Crane, as well as the main, mostly 'cut-and-cover', route for the railway to the airport perimeter. Both Hounslow West and Hatton Cross stations, it was announced, would have island platforms, that at Hounslow West being linked by a covered walkway to the existing ticket hall. At Hatton Cross the ticket hall was to be at surface level with the platforms below the surface.

Work on the extension began on 28 April, with Desmond (now Sir Desmond) Plummer, then Leader of the Greater London Council, operating a tracked excavator to scoop out the first bite of earth for the new tunnel on a site at Hatton Cross. Work on this stage of the extension was expected to take some 3½ years.

The contract for the second stage of the extension, the 1¼ miles of twin deep tube tunnels between Hatton Cross and the centre of the airport, including the construction of a crossover tunnel just before reaching the future site of Heathrow Central Station, was let in December 1971 to John Mowlem & Co. Ltd., at a cost of £2¼ million. Sir William Halcrow & Partners were the consulting engineers. The work, begun early in 1972, was expected to take 2½ years, after which the track would be laid and signalling and other equipment installed.

The contract for the civil engineering work at Heathrow Central station was let to Taylor Woodrow Construction Ltd., the consulting engineers again being Sir William Halcrow & Partners. The station design took into consideration proposals for future development by the British Airports Authority around and above it. The basic structure was to be a reinforced concrete box some 400 ft. long and 80 ft. wide, taken down to below track level. The basic 'box' was to be formed by the bentonite walling system and excavated by conventional methods.

The ticket hall was to be 20 ft. below ground, with the bulk of the staff accommodation being contained on a mezzanine floor some 11 ft. lower, and the platforms 44 ft. down. Two pairs of escalators were to be erected within this box structure to connect platform and ticket hall levels and a two-way escalator and fixed stairs would connect ticket hall and street. Work began at the end of October 1972. The British Airports Authority was to construct subways from the ticket hall with travolator connections to each of its three passenger terminal buildings. At the end of 1974, the 'cut-and-cover' section was complete, as far as civil engineering work was concerned, as were the bored tunnels into the airport itself, and equipment was being installed, track laying was well in hand, and building work was in progress.

In November 1971 an order had been placed with Metro-Cammell Ltd. of Birmingham for the bodies and bogies of 88 new trains for the Piccadilly Line in readiness for the extension to Heathrow Aiport. Contracts for the motors and other equipment were placed with other manufacturers for incorporation in the new trains. The trains were to have six cars instead of the seven of earlier Piccadilly Line trains, but each car would be 58 ft. long compared with just over 51 ft. for the cars then used on the line. They were to have a number of new features, including more space round the doors to allow luggage to be accommodated and a load-weighing system to enable the best use to be made of braking and motor power. They would also have provision for later conversion to automatic operation with a one-man crew. The first train was due for delivery in 1974. They qualified for the government infrastructure grant of 75 per cent of the cost applicable to replacement rolling stock and the balance was met by the Greater London Council.

A special motif, new to the Underground was designed for use on the Piccadilly Line and its trains to call attention to the direct link with the airport. The motif – an aircraft silhouette – was to be incorporated in the 'Heathrow' destination blind on the front of trains and in the 'Heathrow' destination platform indicators throughout the line. The motif came into early use on Underground maps displayed at stations.

Progress on the 'cut-and-cover' section was rapid – so much so that the Piccadilly Line service was extended over the new line to

Hatton Cross from 19 July 1975, giving a four-minute service in peak hours and at least a 10-minute service at other times on weekdays and a 15-minute service on Sundays. The non-stop bus link between Hounslow West and the airport was however retained for the convenience of air travellers.

At the end of 1977 everything came together. All the new trains for the Piccadilly Line had been delivered (though they were not all ready for service), Heathrow Central station in its bright decor was virtually complete, and the final section of the extension was ready for public service. It would be the first time anywhere in the world that a capital city's major international airport would be directly linked to the underground network of its parent city.

On 16 December 1977 Her Majesty the Queen rode in the cab of a special train from Hatton Cross to Heathrow Central and unveiled a memorial plaque. The Heathrow extension was both officially open and open to the public. Air travellers began to 'Fly the Tube' the same day, the first of the 12 million eventually expected to use the line every year. The station at Heathrow is spacious and bright as befits what, to many, is not only the gateway to London, but also to Britain. Its equipment is as modern as its walls, with automatic ticket machines (including a new multi-fare type) and a journey planner which needs only the depression of buttons to show on a television-type screen the route to any other station, in colour, and with interchange points clearly marked (and repeated in words in any of three languages). The train movements into and out of the station are controlled by computer and supervised from the Earl's Court control room.

The proposed fourth terminal at Heathrow could be served by a further extension costing about £20 million (see map on page 156).

Another extension under active consideration in the early 1970s was a revival of an earlier scheme to extend the Bakerloo Line from Elephant & Castle to Camberwell. The scheme, studied in conjunction with the London Borough of Southwark, would have extended the line, via Camberwell Green, to Peckham. Discussions were widened, after a second report had been presented in January 1972 by the joint Council and London Transport working party, to include representatives of the Department of the Environment, the Greater London Council, and British Railways.

Another scheme, mentioned earlier, to extend the Aldwych branch of the Piccadilly Line under the river to Waterloo, could be swallowed up in a new long-term proposal to provide a new south-west to north-east line. This might take over the Wimbledon branch of the District Line (simplifying and therefore improving District Line operation) and then run under Chelsea to Sloane Square and Victoria. From there the alignment would take it to Waterloo, north to Holborn, then north-east to Old Street, Hackney, Leyton, and Leytonstone, with the possibility of taking over the Hainault branch of the Central Line. The exact route is by no means settled and certainly no work on such a line could take place until the 1980s.

The Fleet Line has already been mentioned briefly, but, to recapitulate, it was envisaged that it would take over the Stanmore branch of the Bakerloo Line and then run in new construction from Baker Street via Bond Street, Green Park, Trafalgar Square/Strand, Aldwych, Ludgate Circus, and Cannon Street to Fenchurch Street, continuing to Surrey Docks and over the present East London Line route to New Cross and Lewisham, with a branch from Surrey Docks to New Cross Gate. This would entail cutting back the East London Line service to run between Surrey Docks and Whitechapel/Shoreditch only. There would be a peak hour service of eight-car automatically-operated trains running every two minutes.

During 1970 the Fleet Line proposals were considered by the Greater London Transport Group which was set up under the transport planning provisions of the Transport (London) Act, 1969. The group consisted of representatives of the Department of the Environment, the Greater London Council, the British Railways Board, and London Transport, with the G.L.C. Controller of Planning and Transportation as chairman. A Public Transport and General Committee, a subsidiary of the main group, prepared work for presentation to it.

The Greater London Transport Group came to the opinion that there were strong arguments on planning grounds for building the Fleet Line and that it should terminate at Lewisham rather than New Cross as originally proposed. In view of this, London Transport made formal application in May 1970 to the Greater London Council for authority to build the line, subject to Parliamentary powers being granted for the section from the Strand to Lewisham. Powers for the Baker Street–Strand section had been granted in 1969.

In announcing its application, London Transport stated that it believed that, because of the contribution the new railway would make in helping to solve London's transportation problems, the positive social benefits it would bring, and the part it would play in the London of the future, the capital outlay should be financed from public sources, partly by a government infrastructure grant and partly by a G.L.C. grant. It was accordingly asking the Minister of Transport and the G.L.C. to finance the project.

The new line was estimated to cost £86 million, at 1970 price levels. This figure excluded the cost of some work on the existing system which would be necessary quite apart from the Fleet Line – the reconstruction of Bond Street and Strand stations, and the resignalling of the Stanmore branch of the Bakerloo Line north of Baker Street. The precise siting and cost of the station at Lewisham would be for further consideration by London Transport in consultation with the various authorities concerned, including the London Borough of Lewisham. If work on the Fleet Line were to be started soon, the statement added, the first stage from Stanmore to Strand could be opened in 5½ years.

The Fleet Line was designed to provide interchange with every other Underground line and with British Railways main line terminals at Charing Cross, Cannon Street, and Fenchurch Street. Among the major benefits it could bring is the relief of the serious overcrowding on the most heavily-used section of the whole London Underground network – the Bakerloo Line between Baker Street and Oxford Circus – which is at present carrying 24,000 passengers an hour into the West End during the morning peak and a similar number in the homeward direction in the evening peak. With the Fleet Line taking over the Stanmore branch of the Bakerloo, it would become possible to double the Bakerloo Line service through Paddington on what is now the Queen's Park branch.

The Fleet Line was planned to give London's north-west suburbs a direct link with the City and to provide a large area of south-east London with a fast direct service to the heart of the City and West End. The importance of the new link it could give with the south-east is heightened by the major housing developments planned for the Surrey Docks and Deptford areas. Some of the load on the Southern Region's hard-pressed south-eastern sector could be lifted at a time when, otherwise, the developing new town of Thamesmead would create further problems. (Parliamentary powers for the Strand–New Cross section were granted in 1971 and those for the New Cross–Lewisham section in 1972.)

The Greater London Council approved the Fleet Line scheme in July 1970, agreeing to meet 25 per cent of the capital outlay provided that the Government agreed to make a 75 per cent infrastructure grant for the remainder. A formal application was made and on 18 August 1971 Peter Walker, Secretary of State for the Environment, announced at a press conference held in London Transport's Northern and Victoria lines divisional headquarters at Cobourg Street, Euston, that the Government would pay 75 per cent of the £35 million (at mid-1971 prices) cost of Stage I of the Fleet Line (Baker Street to Trafalgar Square/Strand). Simultaneously London Transport announced that its plans for the line were well advanced and preliminary work would begin in a few weeks. The first sign, it stated, would be work in Oxford Street near Bond Street station to locate pipes, cables, and other services as a preliminary to building a temporary steel deck over the site of the enlarged ticket hall concourse. Work began on this site on 29 September 1971, only six weeks after the announcement. The first main site was on the vacant ground at the side of the National Gallery, where two 100-ft. shafts were sunk. From these, access tunnels passed under Trafalgar Square to enable the running tunnels to be built between Admiralty Arch and Aldwych.

This £2½ million contract was awarded to Kinnear Moodie & Co. Ltd. and involved driving and lining about half a mile of twin tube tunnels. It included platform tunnels for the Fleet Line at the combined Strand/Trafalgar Square station and a 30-ft diameter crossover tunnel west of the station. The tunnels east of the station would run to a point below the Strand/Lancaster Place road junction (Aldwych), and be used initially as sidings, becoming part of the through Fleet Line route to the City and beyond at a later date when further stages of the new tube were authorized.

Also included in the contract, which was expected to take about 2½ years to complete, was a low-level concourse between the Fleet Line platforms at the Strand/Trafalgar Square station, with cross passages and two escalator shafts. One of these would lead up to the landing at the bottom of the existing Trafalgar Square Bakerloo Line escalators, the other to a new intermediate concourse at Strand Northern Line station.

The first 2½-mile section of the Fleet Line was planned to give interchange with seven existing Underground lines – the Bakerloo and Northern lines at Strand/Trafalgar Square; the Bakerloo,

Metropolitan, and Circle Lines at Baker Street; the Central at Bond Street; and the Piccadilly and Victoria at Green Park.

The next site to be used had been 'mothballed' since the completion of the Victoria Line – the site in Piccadilly on the edge of Green Park. It became the base for driving running tunnels in both directions – towards Admiralty Arch and Bond Street. The contract for this 1½-mile section was let to A. Waddington & Son Ltd. It included the Fleet Line platform tunnels at Green Park station and was expected to take about 2½ years to complete. The third main working site was at Park Crescent, behind Regent's Park station.

The running tunnels between Baker Street and Bond Street were built by Charles Brand & Son Ltd., whose contract covered the construction of the twin running tunnels as well as a junction with the southbound Bakerloo Line Stanmore branch below British Railways Marylebone Station. Sir William Halcrow & Partners were the consulting engineers for this section.

At Baker Street one new station tunnel and platform were needed – parallel to the existing northbound Bakerloo Line platform. This would make it possible to provide interchange at the same level between the northbound services on the Bakerloo and Fleet Lines. In the southbound direction trains from the two branches already have separate platforms so that Fleet Line trains would use the Stanmore branch platform – giving cross-platform interchange with the southbound Bakerloo Line. The new station tunnel, together with a short length of running tunnel connecting with the existing northbound Bakerloo Line Stanmore branch tunnel north of the station, with various interchange subways and ventilation and cable tunnels, was to be built by John Mowlem & Co. Ltd., with Sir William Halcrow & Partners as consulting engineers.

The first part of the Fleet Line runs mostly in the London clay which has served the Underground so well, but in deeper sections it is likely to penetrate the more variable Woolwich and Reading beds.

At Bond Street the course of the Fleet Line is below the Central Line and at right-angles to it. There are to be escalator connections between the two lines for interchange and two new escalators are to link the newly-enlarged ticket hall with the Central Line level; the existing escalators are being retained and modernized.

The civil engineering work at Bond Street was carried out under a £2½ million contract by Balfour, Beatty & Co. Ltd. with Messrs. Mott, Hay & Anderson as consulting engineers. It is expected that the opening of the Fleet Line will increase the number of passengers using this station from 12 million to 20 million a year. The first major task of the constructors was to build an 'umbrella' bridge over the road junction by the station to allow work on the new ticket hall to be carried out below without interfering with road traffic. The bridge – or 'deck' – was built during the Late Summer Bank Holiday weekend in 1972.

Green Park will provide interchange with both Victoria and Piccadilly lines. The Trafalgar Square/Strand station, already described, is to be renamed 'Charing Cross', and the station of that name by the river became 'Charing Cross–Embankment' on 4 August 1974 and 'Embankment' on 12 September 1976.

To allow work on the new station to go on beneath the forecourt of the main line station at Charing Cross, a steel decking was erected during the Easter weekend of 1973 (leaving the Queen Eleanor Cross undisturbed) and after the last train on 16 June, Strand station was closed for rebuilding. The closure was necessary because the new escalator shafts were to be built through the earlier lift shafts. The station will reopen in its new form when the first stage of the Fleet Line comes into operation.

The main Fleet Line rolling stock depot – provided that the rest of the line is authorized – is to be at Surrey Docks, but in order that the first stage of the Fleet Line can be brought into use, another rolling stock depot has had to be found. This is to be Neasden depot, which formerly housed Metropolitan and Bakerloo Line trains. To make room for the new stock, a new depot has been built at Stonebridge Park, near the London Midland Region depot, to accommodate the displaced Bakerloo Line stock. The only access for trains to this new depot is via the LMR tracks.

The first stage of the Fleet Line (which is to be silver-grey on London Transport's Underground maps) is just over 13¾ miles long (including the Stanmore Branch) and will have 17 stations. The through running time will probably be 36 minutes. In the last few years, however, there have been many developments in the Fleet Line story.

The running tunnels between Baker Street and Strand were finished by the end of 1974 and work on the stations was going ahead. Both London Transport and the Greater London Council were by then pressing the Government for financial support for the second stage of the Fleet Line, which would take it on to Fenchurch Street. Quite apart from the natural desire to keep the engineering teams together to get on with the job, there were fears that new buildings with deep foundations might obstruct the chosen route. The Government would not move, however, until the London Rail Study then in progress (see later) had been completed. After the report was published the Department of the Environment declared that the building of Stage 2 to Fenchurch Street, and sections onward through Dockland (referred to as the 'River Line') would depend largely for justification on their role in helping to redevelop Dockland. This would therefore have to wait until 1976, when decisions would be taken on the Docklands plan as a whole. The London Docklands Strategic Plan, published in July 1976, strongly supported the Underground line, but no Government money was forthcoming in that year. Meanwhile, planning for the River Line between Fenchurch Street and Custom House went on with a view to making application for Parliamentary powers in 1978. East of Custom House, the line would run to Thamesmead, but while London Transport and the G.L.C. favoured a route via Woolwich, the Docklands Joint Committee were torn between this route and one which would take the River Line via Beckton.

In mid-1977, the year of Her Majesty the Queen's Jubilee, the G.L.C. decided that the Fleet and River Lines should cease to exist as such and should be known instead as the Jubilee Line. Though other work was well in hand and parts of it, notably the new (upper) escalators at Bond Street, were in use by the end of 1977, there was a long delay in the contractor's work on escalators. The opening date of Stage I had to be put back again, this time until late 1978.

The Government still would not provide finance for Stage 2, but the G.L.C. were considering bearing the cost alone if necessary. Some work had already been carried out at various sites with the object of preserving the route. Planning proceeded on the rest of the line on the assumption that the route would run via Millwall, Custom House, Silvertown and Woolwich, ending at Thamesmead: Beckton would be served by a branch from Custom House (see map on p. 157). A site for the Jubilee Line train depot was found at Beckton and agreed with the local authorities.

At the time of writing it appeared that the first stage of the Jubilee Line was unlikely to open before early 1979, though most work was completed and trains started to run into the new tunnels (for training purposes only) from mid-August 1978. The details of the stations, with their imaginative colour schemes, will no doubt be widely described when the line is opened but must await the next edition of this book.

London's Underground is truly moving into a new age with the Victoria Line a proved success, the Heathrow extension in full commission and growing daily in popularity, and the first section of the Jubilee Line almost on the point of opening. But in planning new lines there is no intention of neglecting the old. The Victoria Line set new standards and many plans are already prepared – and others are on the way – to, as far as money and resources permit, bring the rest of the Underground up to Victoria Line standards or better. This is not something which can be done overnight, and much of it will undoubtedly be linked with the building of new lines – just as Oxford Circus station was completely remodelled in connection with the Victoria Line and Bond Street is being enlarged and greatly improved at the same time as the Jubilee Line is being built. The full work at Bond Street was due to cost £3.8 million, of which the Government was meeting £2.4 million and the Greater London Council the remainder. The need for the work, apart from the new demands of the Jubilee Line, can be judged from the fact that, before the present work began, Bond Street – in the heart of the West End shopping area – had not been improved for 52 years. Too many other stations are long overdue for improvement – but improvements cost money. A flexible programme has been drawn up which will be kept under constant review as circumstances change, but even in 1974 it called for expenditure of well upwards of £400 million during the following 20 years.

The first fruits of this up-dating are already to be seen at Victoria, where the District and Circle Line platforms have been brought to Victoria Line standards. Similar work has transformed Old Street and South Kensington, and other stations already completed or in the pipe-line for improvements are Archway, Bank, Blackfriars, Cannon Street, Debden, Embankment, Finsbury Park, Holloway, Ladbroke Grove, Piccadilly Circus, Russell Square, Stockwell, Tottenham Court Road and Waterloo, with minor work at many others.

Escalators, too, are being modernized, and an £850,000 programme – of which the Government is meeting half the cost – is dealing with older machines at Charing Cross, Clapham Common, Clapham North, Liverpool Street, Old Street, and Oxford Circus. Signalling improvements include the alteration of the Northern Line equipment to programme machine control with central supervision from the Cobourg Street control room, and there is a continuing programme of other changes.

The rolling stock programme has largely already been dealt with in connection with new lines, but one important change not yet noted is on the Northern Line, which is receiving all the 'silver' trains from the Piccadilly Line as that line gets its new trains. With the 30 completely new trains already built especially for it, costing £8½ million, this was intended to give the Northern Line a modern all-silver fleet, and in fact the last "red" train in normal passenger service on the Northern Line ran on 14 April 1978. The 33 trains built to run on the Northern Line to fill the gap until all the Piccadilly Line trains can be transferred will be available to operate the first stage of the Jubilee Line. They are capable of being converted to automatic one-man operation. Provided proposals that in the later stages the Jubilee Line will be worked by trains of a new and advanced design are implemented – and preliminary studies of the stock have for some time been at a stage where a prototype could be built – the 33 trains will then be transferred again – to the Bakerloo Line, so enabling the last of the 1938 tube stock to be withdrawn. Meanwhile, many of the seven-car trains of 1938 stock operating on the Northern and Bakerloo Lines are being overhauled and refurbished for further service on the Bakerloo Line. The District Line was not neglected. In 1976 11 new six-car trains were placed on order for the Edgware Road–Putney Bridge service (C.77 stock). These resembled the new trains already in use for the Circle and Hammersmith & City services and were delivered in 1977/78. Design work was also put in hand for a new type of stock to replace the ageing main District Line fleet. This work was almost completed and first orders placed for 75 new six-car trains in 1976, with deliveries expected to begin in 1978. Final design work was finished and the remaining orders placed in 1977. It is to be known as D.78 stock. Because of the need for economy, the air suspension originally intended for this stock is being replaced by a new design using solid rubber. Other features include four single-leaf doors on each side of the car. These will be opened by passengers pressing a button, but closed by the guard. The rise in the use of 'chopper' control of traction equipment has been closely followed by London Transport's engineers, who have done their own tests with it. The outcome is that two experimental three-car units with this type of control were obtained and are being tested on the Central Line. Among other advantages of the system, the equipment enables the electrical energy created by braking forces to be fed back into the track for use by other trains. Such energy is normally dissipated by the use of resistances.

Another rolling stock development was the ordering, in 1972, of eleven new battery locomotives to supplement the then existing fleet of 35 such locomotives, which can run either from the line rails, or, when current has been taken off the rails for engineering work, from their large storage batteries.

The up-dating plan also includes elements not so obvious to passengers – except from their results. One of the major aims is to achieve even greater reliability in train operation. This entails the removal of bottlenecks and track layouts which hinder good train working and improving communications and control systems to the most modern standards. In the past, trains have sometimes been kept in depots when they should be running the peak-hour service because a derailment at the depot entrance has prevented their running out on to the main line. Depots, as far as possible, will now be provided with more than one exit to the running tracks and trains will be protected from the severe winter weather which can freeze, or block with snow and ice, essential running gear. It is intended that computers will be used to assist in the control of train operation and a start has been made on this, notably, as already mentioned, at Heathrow, and on the Northern and Victoria Lines. Another important field of enterprise is in the reduction of Underground train noise as heard by the passenger – something which trials elsewhere in the world have shown to be very difficult to achieve.

Many bridges also are being replaced or renewed and others are being built or rebuilt in connection with road improvements. The largest is a pre-stressed concrete bridge with a span of 152 ft. which carries the Central Line over the new M.11 motorway between Chigwell and Roding Valley stations. Station lighting is being improved as opportunities permit, one large scheme being one begun in 1972 to improve the lighting at 12 Northern Line stations on the section south of the Thames. This included the complete re-lighting of Clapham Common and Tooting Broadway stations.

An important change in policy relating to automatic ticket gates came in 1972 when, after studying the results of automatic fare collection trials on the Victoria Line, London Transport decided that efforts for the ensuing five years would be concentrated on providing the comparatively simple inwards-only automatic gates at stations. These are more reliable and less expensive than the much more complicated exit-gate equipment (which has to perform many checks before accepting a ticket as valid) and do ensure that every passenger entering the system has a valid ticket of some kind. With losses from fare evasion running at up to £8 million a year this aspect was regarded as particularly important. A further step, as the automatic gates, are introduced, has been to equip many of the manual ticket inspection inwards barriers (used mainly by season ticket holders) with gates similar to the automatic ones but operated by the ticket collector who is provided with an actuating pedal. Prototype gates of this type were installed at Seven Sisters station in 1972 and others were fitted early in 1974 at Leicester Square.

One difficulty has always been that if a ticket office has been shut – in the case of a booking clerk falling ill, for example, and there being no replacement available – passengers enter the system without a ticket of any kind. Now, however, arrangements are in hand, through special machines or otherwise, to ensure that every passenger can at least purchase a minimum fare ticket. Special ticket machines, painted red, selling 10p 'authority to travel' tickets when for any reason the booking office is closed, were brought into use at 13 stations on 4 December 1977. Passengers holding these tickets pay any excess fare at their destination. All arrangements will be such that they will fit in with automatic exit gates when installed at a future date. Meanwhile, the automatic outwards gates fitted at 22 stations have already been removed and transferred for duty as inwards gates elsewhere. In 1974 the Greater London Council agreed that automatic 'inwards' gates should be installed at the majority of London Transport stations not already so equipped, at a cost of some £10 million – this cost being recovered from extra receipts arising from the much greater degree of control and deterrent to fraud given by the system.

When most stations have inwards gates it should be possible for passengers to buy tickets printed and encoded with the fare value and type of ticket only. These would not be dated and could thus be sold either singly or in bulk and could be used for a journey costing the face value from any station, giving a considerable degree of flexibility. These tickets would automatically be impressed with the date and the name of the station where the passenger started his journey as they were put into the inwards gate, a process which would automatically cancel them. The ticket collector could then check, at the end of the journey, that the ticket was valid for that particular journey and that the correct fare had been paid. Single tickets sold in bulk might have a price reduction sufficient to compare with that for weekly season tickets, making it possible to discontinue the sale of weekly seasons though retaining those valid for one month or longer.

This is not to say that the idea of a complete automatic fare collection system has been abandoned – it has not, and in June 1978 London Transport sought authority from the Greater London Council to take the first steps towards such a scheme, estimated to cost £55 million. But the complication of the outwards gates – and the other station equipment which goes with them and performs the actual checking cannot be justified for the time being while so many tickets still being issued are not coded for automatic fare collection. This applies particularly to tickets issued from British Railways stations, though it is hoped that a compatible joint system can be worked out.

Something has already been said of London Transport's plans for further new Underground lines, but in 1971 a large-scale survey was begun which, over a period of several months, distributed questionnaire cards to many thousands of passengers asking for details of their journeys from particular stations. The answers to all these have been processed to yield information which will be of great help in planning the future development of, and extensions to, the Underground system.

Other planning developments included the commissioning by London Transport in 1972 of a study into the possible benefits to environment in London which could stem from better integration of major planning and redevelopment schemes with public transport. The area chosen for the study was that affected by the third stage of the Fleet Line, i.e. between Fenchurch Street and Lewisham. The study was undertaken by Messrs. Llewelyn-Davies, Weeks, Forestier-Walker & Bor, and, when completed, showed the benefit of a new Underground line in encouraging development or redevelopment of the area the line would serve.

A further study to form the basis for planning the future of rail facilities in London was set up jointly by the Department of the Environment, the Greater London Council, British Railways, and London Transport under the chairmanship of Sir David Barran. The report, Part I of which was published in November 1974, went to the Secretary of State for the Environment. Part II was published the following year. The report, after dealing with the then current staffing problems, made it clear that it considered the first priority should be the maintenance in a state of full efficiency of the then existing Underground and British Rail commuter systems. Only then came improvements and extensions. A twenty-five year period – from 1975 to the end of the century – was discussed and it is significant that although three plans were considered, costing from £2,000 to £2,400 million, in each case some £1,400 million was set aside for the maintenance of the existing system, thus emphasizing the importance – and the cost – of the maintenance and renewal work which is so often taken for granted.

As far as Underground developments were concerned, the report was in favour of building Stage 2 of the Fleet Line from Strand to Fenchurch Street and continuing it as what it termed the 'River Line' to Woolwich and Thamesmead (Both the 'Fleet' and 'River' lines have since been superseded – in name at least – by the 'Jubilee' Line, as already explained). The report supported the making of an early start on Stage 2 of the Fleet Line. The report gave lower priority to the Chelsea–Hackney line (part of the south-west–north-east route already described from Wimbledon to Hainault) and to the extension of the Fleet Line to Lewisham and possibly the Hayes/Addiscombe area. The report did not recommend the extension of the Bakerloo Line to Camberwell and Peckham which, as recorded elsewhere, had been under discussion for some time.

The report also recommended the setting-up of a new rail advisory committee with the Department of the Environment, British Railways, the Greater London Council and London Transport all represented. The chairman, however, should be independent of any of these bodies. Accordingly, the formation of the London Rail Advisory Committee was announced in October 1976. It is expected to have a wide co-ordinating influence on many matters, including fares. In addition, a new liaison body was set up by British Railways and London Transport to strengthen working arrangements between them.

In 1977 the finance for Stage 2 of the Jubilee Line seemed as far off as ever, but 'stop-gap' proposals which would improve Dockland travel and attract Government funds earmarked for 'Inner City' areas were formulated. These provided for the construction of a new station on the Stratford – North Woolwich line of British Railways at West Ham to give direct interchange with the District and Hammersmith & City Lines of London Transport, and for the modernization of other stations on the Stratford – North Woolwich line. Stations on the East London Line were also to be improved under this scheme and the Greater London Council was being asked to consider other improvements to the line, including the reconstruction of the station at Surrey Docks. Consideration was also being given to the building of the Custom House – Woolwich section of the Jubilee Line in advance of the rest of the line being approved.

Tunnelling through unstable ground has always presented difficulties, causing more than one hold-up during the construction of the Victoria Line, but London Transport, in association with the National Research and Development Corporation, has sponsored the development of a new type of tunnelling shield which, in the course of constructing a 200 yd. tunnel in South East London near New Cross on the route of the Jubilee Line, showed distinct possibilities and excited the interest of engineers from many parts of the world. The principle involved is the pumping of a bentonite clay slurry into a sealed cutting head compartment at the front of the shield. The clay has thixotropic qualities and forms a 'skin' on the face ahead of the shield, the 'skin' being sufficient to keep it from collapsing before there is time to insert the rings of tunnel lining segments.

The carrier-wave system used for driver-controller communication on the Victoria Line, though a great advance on anything available before, proved to have certain limitations, especially when trains were close together. The use of radio seemed obvious, but radio waves do not carry far in Tube tunnels, and any system had to be effective in all kinds of tunnels, in cuttings, and in the open air. Experiments were carried out on the Bakerloo Line using a 'radiating cable' to carry the radio transmissions and this proved so successful that it was decided to use the system, with booster amplifiers spaced along the cables, throughout the Bakerloo and Fleet (now Jubilee) line tunnels. The radio operates normally in the open air. In 1978, London Transport sought GLC approval to extend radio control to the Northern Line and it is hoped eventually to extend it to the whole of the Underground.

With the many new lines now being proposed for the Underground it is strange to have to record the loss of one which penetrates to the heart of the City – though it has been lost only to London Transport and is now enjoying perhaps the busiest period of its life and fulfilling the purpose for which it was originally built some 70 years before. The Highbury Branch of the Northern Line closed on 7 September 1975 and was handed over to British Railways to become part of their newly-electrified Great Northern suburban network. Trains from Welwyn Garden City and Hertford North now run via a new link from Finsbury Park to Drayton Park and on to Moorgate, giving interchange with the Underground at Finsbury Park, Highbury & Islington, Old Street, and Moorgate.

It is matter for deep regret that in the last months of London Transport control this line saw the worst accident ever to occur on the Underground when, on 28 February 1975, a passenger train ran at high speed into the end wall of the terminal station at Moorgate with the loss of over 40 lives. Since then, a £1 million programme of speed control and other safety measures has been put in hand at terminal stations to make sure, as far as is possible, that such a disaster can never occur again.

The switching of the Eastern Region Moorgate trains to the Highbury branch left their former peak-hour route to Moorgate via the Widened Lines deserted except for a very small number of London Midland Region trains. This situation will be changed by British Railways £80 million scheme to electrify the Bedford–St. Pancras/Moorgate lines, when up to 12 trains an hour will use the newly-electrified Widened Lines. As part of this scheme, the station in Pentonville Road now called King's Cross is to be renamed King's Cross Midland. It will be completely rebuilt and linked by subway to London Transport's King's Cross–St. Pancras station. The new complex will come into use with the electrified services in 1982.

The increasing role played by women on the Underground is perhaps most strikingly marked by the appointment of Mrs. Ann Dadds as the first woman train driver in October 1978. She had already worked for seven months as a guard.

And finally, a note of nostalgia. The last day of steam locomotive operation on London Transport was celebrated on 6 June 1971 by a commemorative run by a steam-hauled train from Moorgate to Neasden depot. Made up of engineers' rolling stock headed by one of London Transport's last three 0-6-0 pannier tank locomotives, L.94, it was watched by two thousand enthusiasts as it passed from Moorgate through Barbican and Farringdon stations. They then followed it to Neasden in four electric trains.

At Neasden, the locomotive and train were on view to the public as part of an open day at the depot. Other exhibits included one of the three Rolls-Royce/Sentinel 325 h.p. diesel hydraulic 0-6-0 locomotives which have replaced the three steam locomotives (L.90, L.94, and L.95) for hauling works trains and for shunting duties.

The Museum of British Transport at Clapham closed in April 1972, but London Transport decided that its collection of historical vehicles, etc., should not go to York with the British Railways exhibits but should remain in the city they had served. After a considerable search for suitable premises, a new home for the Underground trains – as well as buses, trams, and trolleybuses – was found at Syon Park, Brentford, where a large pavilion was adapted to hold what was officially named the 'London Transport Collection'. The Collection was opened on 23 May 1973 by the Duke of Northumberland, within whose estate the pavilion lies. The Collection will move again in 1979 to the old Flower Market at Covent Garden. In this Central London location it will be enlarged and improved, becoming the London Transport Museum.

Underground railways are the most rapid practical means of moving masses of people in crowded London. They do it without occupying valuable land, without causing obstruction, and without causing any loss of amenity. Wherever the railways run Londoners are guaranteed rapid transport and, as other countries have found, a rise in the value of land and property. Good communications and swift travel are vital to the life of a city. In the Underground Londoners have a service which has led the world since 1863 and which is still sought out for advice by cities building underground railways in all parts of the world. London's Underground must grow to have new life for itself and for the people of the great city which it serves.

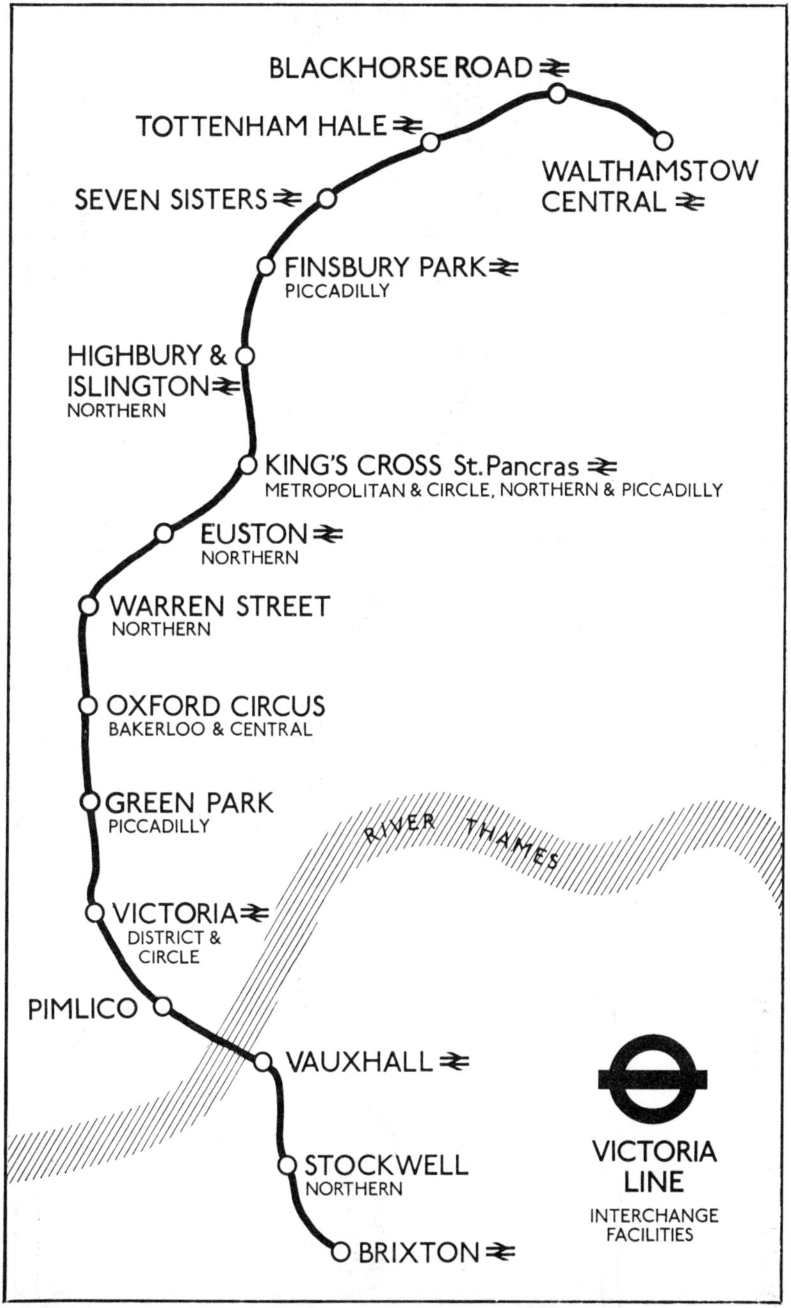
BLACKHORSE ROAD
TOTTENHAM HALE
SEVEN SISTERS
WALTHAMSTOW CENTRAL
FINSBURY PARK
PICCADILLY
HIGHBURY & ISLINGTON
NORTHERN
KING'S CROSS St. Pancras
METROPOLITAN & CIRCLE, NORTHERN & PICCADILLY
EUSTON
NORTHERN
WARREN STREET
NORTHERN
OXFORD CIRCUS
BAKERLOO & CENTRAL
GREEN PARK
PICCADILLY
RIVER THAMES
VICTORIA
DISTRICT & CIRCLE
PIMLICO
VAUXHALL
STOCKWELL
NORTHERN
BRIXTON
VICTORIA LINE
INTERCHANGE FACILITIES

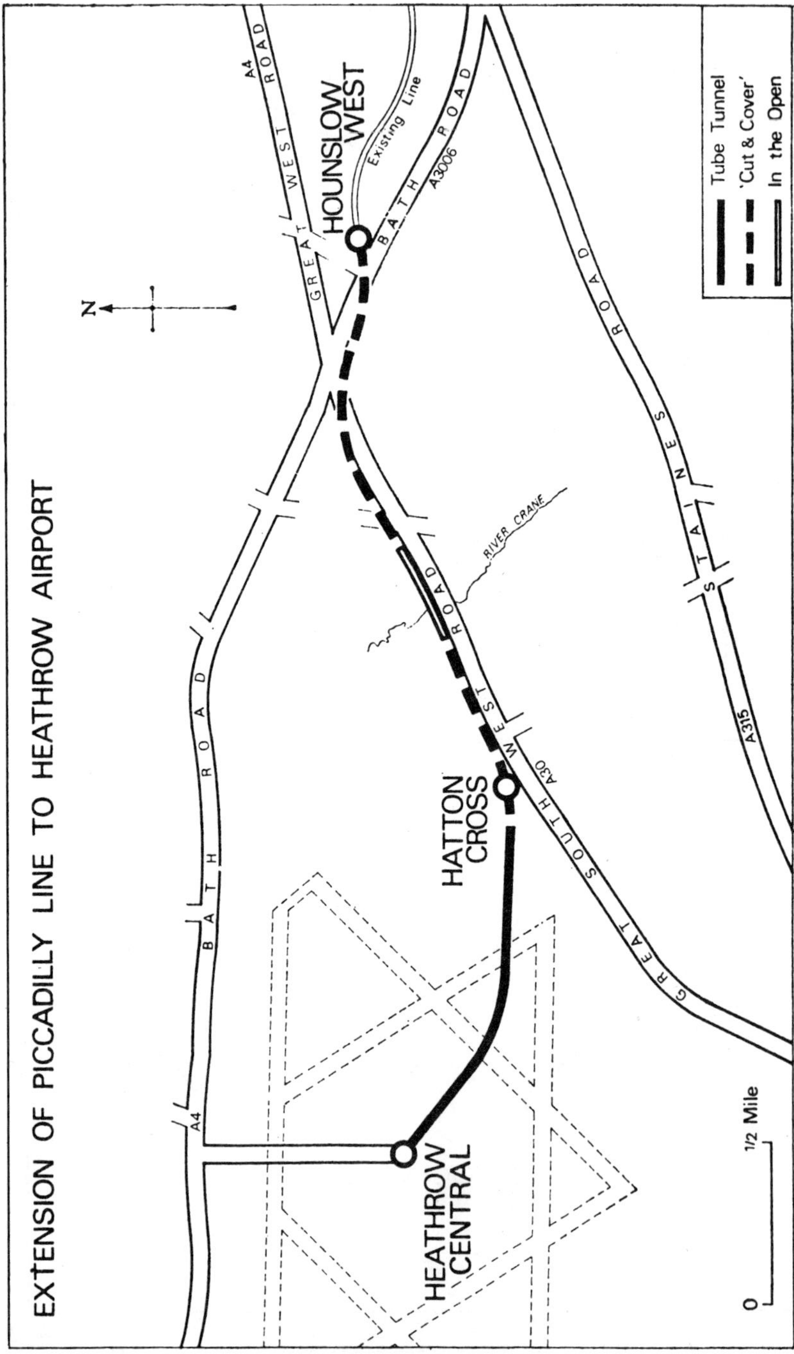
EXTENSION OF PICCADILLY LINE TO HEATHROW AIRPORT
N
HOUNSLOW WEST
HATTON CROSS
HEATHROW CENTRAL
A4
GREAT WEST ROAD
BATH ROAD
A3006
Existing Line
RIVER CRANE
GREAT SOUTH WEST ROAD
A30
STAINES ROAD
A315
Tube Tunnel
'Cut & Cover'
In the Open
0
1/2 Mile
CDS-S-1492

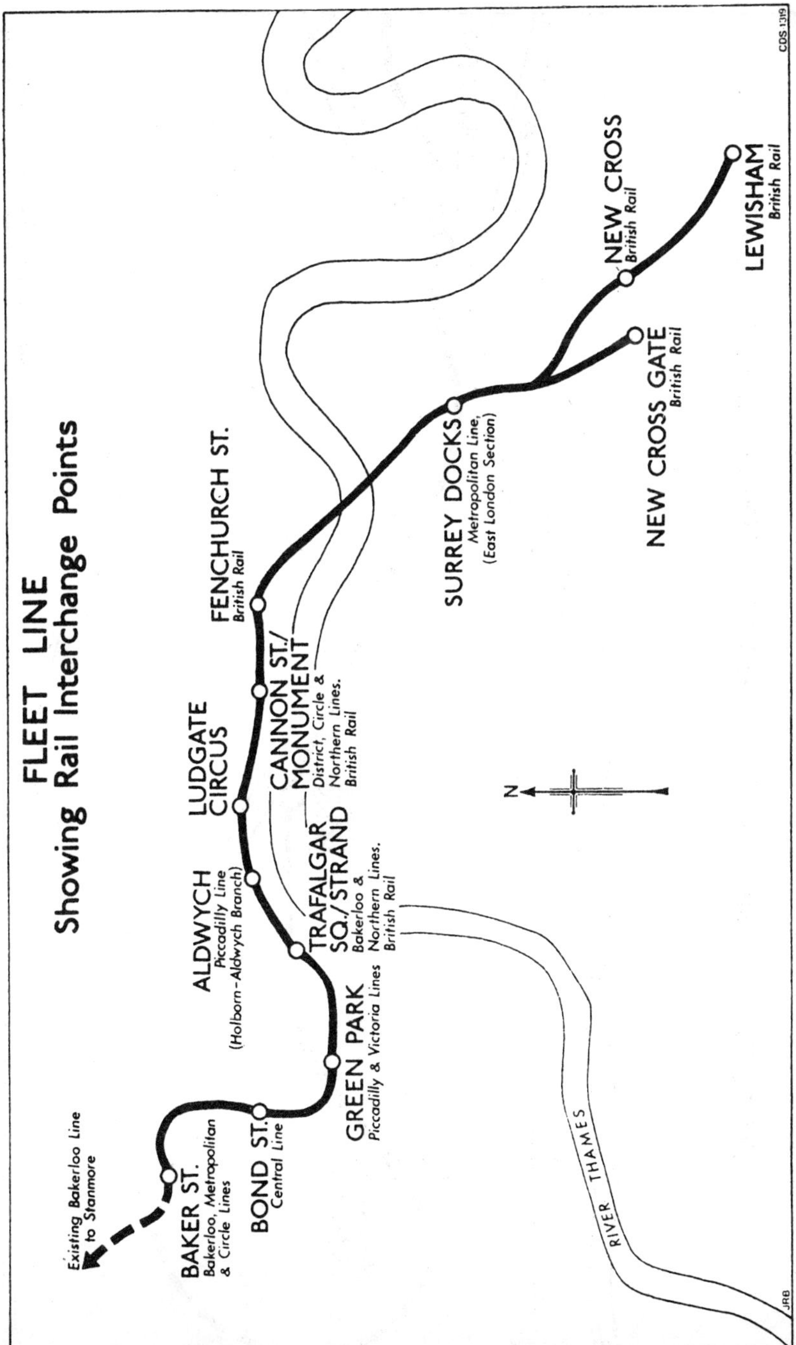
FLEET LINE
Showing Rail Interchange Points
Existing Bakerloo Line to Stanmore
BAKER ST.
Bakerloo, Metropolitan & Circle Lines
BOND ST.
Central Line
GREEN PARK
Piccadilly & Victoria Lines
TRAFALGAR SQ./STRAND
Bakerloo & Northern Lines. British Rail
ALDWYCH
Piccadilly Line (Holborn-Aldwych Branch)
LUDGATE CIRCUS
CANNON ST./ MONUMENT
District, Circle & Northern Lines. British Rail
FENCHURCH ST.
British Rail
SURREY DOCKS
Metropolitan Line, (East London Section)
NEW CROSS GATE
British Rail
NEW CROSS
British Rail
LEWISHAM
British Rail
RIVER THAMES
N
CDS 1319
JRB

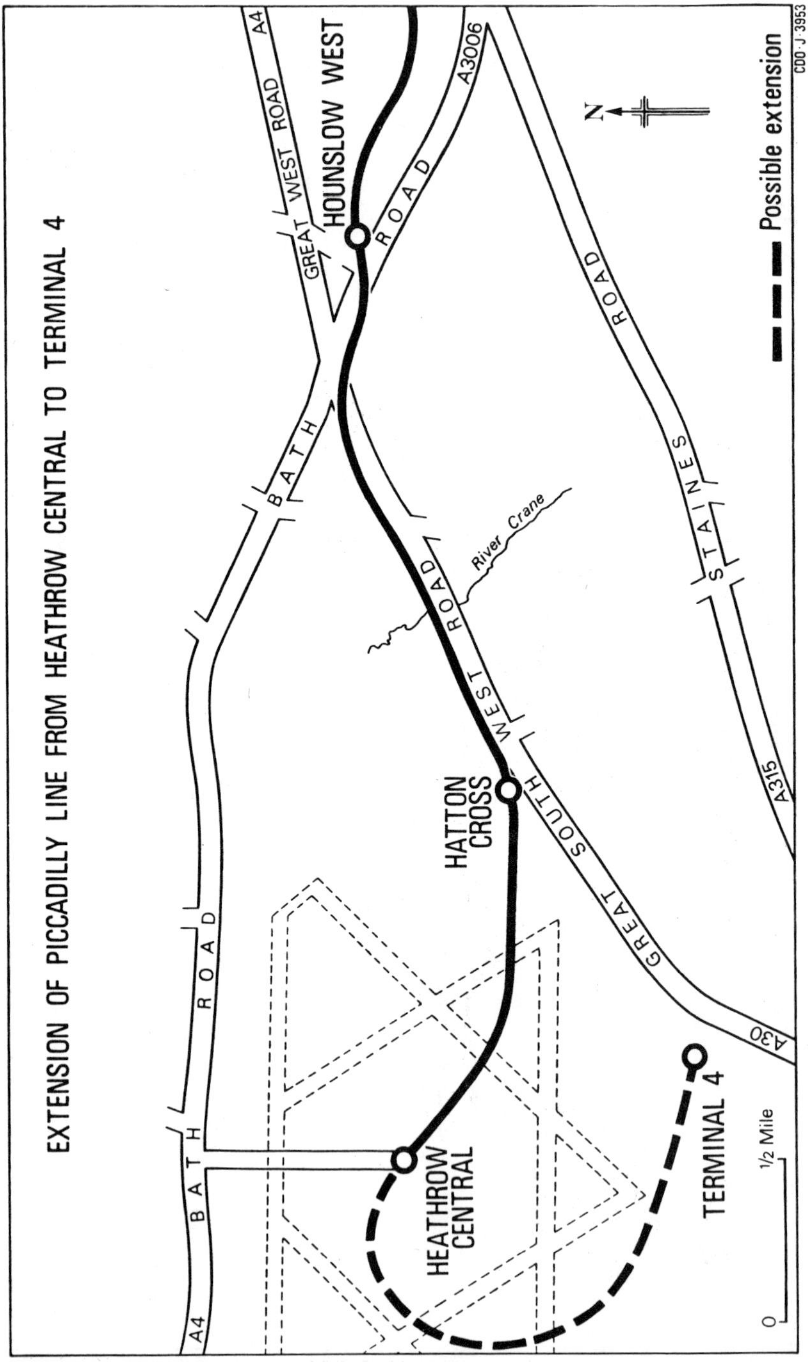
EXTENSION OF PICCADILLY LINE FROM HEATHROW CENTRAL TO TERMINAL 4
HOUNSLOW WEST
HATTON CROSS
HEATHROW CENTRAL
TERMINAL 4
GREAT WEST ROAD
A4
BATH ROAD
A3006
ROAD
GREAT SOUTH WEST ROAD
STAINES ROAD
A315
A30
River Crane
N
Possible extension
0
1/2 Mile
CDO · J · 3953

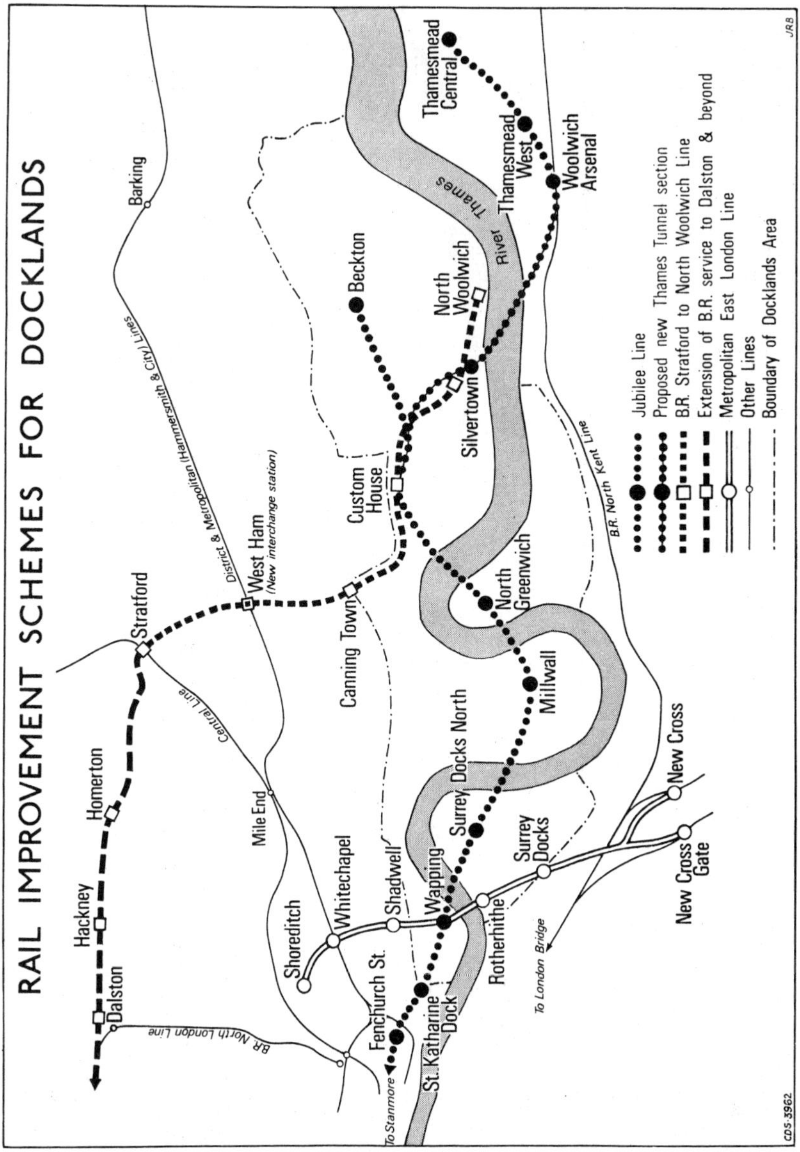
RAIL IMPROVEMENT SCHEMES FOR DOCKLANDS
Jubilee Line
Proposed new Thames Tunnel section
B.R. Stratford to North Woolwich Line
Extension of B.R. service to Dalston & beyond
Metropolitan East London Line
Other Lines
Boundary of Docklands Area
Dalston
Hackney
Homerton
Stratford
Barking
West Ham
(New interchange station)
District & Metropolitan (Hammersmith & City) Lines
Central Line
Mile End
B.R. North London Line
Shoreditch
Whitechapel
Shadwell
Wapping
Fenchurch St.
St. Katharine Dock
To Stanmore
Rotherhithe
To London Bridge
Surrey Docks
Surrey Docks North
New Cross Gate
New Cross
Canning Town
Custom House
Beckton
Silvertown
North Woolwich
North Greenwich
Millwall
River Thames
Thamesmead Central
Thamesmead West
Woolwich Arsenal
B.R. North Kent Line
JRB
CDS 3962

INDEX

1178/211RP/5M(A)

THE LONDON UNDERGROUND
AMERSHAM
CHESHAM
WATFORD
CHALFONT & LATIMER
CROXLEY
CHORLEYWOOD
RICKMANSWORTH
MOOR PARK
NORTHWOOD
NORTHWOOD HILLS
PINNER
WEST RUISLIP
RUISLIP MANOR
RAYNERS LANE
NORTH HARROW
HILLINGDON
UXBRIDGE
ICKENHAM
RUISLIP
EASTCOTE
WEST HARROW
RUISLIP GARDENS
SOUTH RUISLIP
SOUTH HARROW
SUDBURY HILL
SUDBURY TOWN
NORTHOLT
GREENFORD
ALPERTON
PERIVALE
HANGER LANE
PARK ROYAL
NORTH EALING
EALING BROADWAY
EALING COMMON
SOUTH EALING
NORTHFIELDS
BOSTON MANOR
OSTERLEY
HOUNSLOW EAST
HOUNSLOW CENTRAL
HEATHROW CENTRAL
HATTON CROSS
HOUNSLOW WEST
ACTON TOWN
CHISWICK PARK
TURNHAM GREEN
STAMFORD BROOK
RAVENSCOURT PARK
GUNNERSBURY
KEW GARDENS
RICHMOND
SOUTH ACTON
ACTON CENTRAL
WEST ACTON
NORTH ACTON
EAST ACTON
WATFORD JUNCTION
WATFORD HIGH STREET
BUSHEY
CARPENDERS PARK
HATCH END
HEADSTONE LANE
HARROW & WEALDSTONE
HARROW ON THE HILL
KENTON
NORTHWICK PARK
PRESTON ROAD
SOUTH KENTON
NORTH WEMBLEY
WEMBLEY CENTRAL
STONEBRIDGE PARK
HARLESDEN
WILLESDEN JUNCTION
KENSAL RISE
BRONDESBURY
BRONDESBURY PARK
KENSAL GREEN
QUEEN'S PARK
KILBURN PARK
MAIDA VALE
WARWICK AVENUE
ROYAL OAK
WESTBOURNE PARK
LADBROKE GROVE
LATIMER ROAD
WHITE CITY
SHEPHERD'S BUSH
GOLDHAWK ROAD
HAMMERSMITH
BARONS COURT
KENSINGTON (OLYMPIA)
WEST KENSINGTON
EARL'S COURT
WEST BROMPTON
FULHAM BROADWAY
PARSONS GREEN
PUTNEY BRIDGE
EAST PUTNEY
SOUTHFIELDS
WIMBLEDON PARK
WIMBLEDON
STANMORE
CANONS PARK
QUEENSBURY
KINGSBURY
WEMBLEY PARK
NEASDEN
DOLLIS HILL
WILLESDEN GREEN
KILBURN
WEST HAMPSTEAD
FINCHLEY ROAD
SWISS COTTAGE
ST JOHN'S WOOD
FINCHLEY ROAD & FROGNAL
North London Line
EDGWARE
BURNT OAK
COLINDALE
HENDON CENTRAL
BRENT CROSS
GOLDERS GREEN
HAMPSTEAD
HAMPSTEAD HEATH
BELSIZE PARK
CHALK FARM
GOSPEL OAK
CAMDEN TOWN
MORNINGTON CRESCENT
HOLLAND PARK
NOTTING HILL GATE
QUEENSWAY
LANCASTER GATE
MARBLE ARCH
BOND STREET
OXFORD CIRCUS
PADDINGTON
BAYSWATER
EDGWARE ROAD
MARYLEBONE
BAKER STREET
REGENT'S PARK
GREAT PORTLAND STREET
EUSTON
WARREN STREET
EUSTON SQUARE
GOODGE STREET
HIGH STREET KENSINGTON
GLOUCESTER ROAD
SOUTH KENSINGTON
KNIGHTSBR DGE
HYDE PARK CORNER
GREEN PARK
PICCADILLY CIRCUS
SLOANE SQUARE
VICTORIA
PIMLICO
ST JAMES'S PARK
WESTMINSTER
CHARING CROSS
EMBANKMENT
Charing Cross
TOTTENHAM COURT ROAD
COVENT GARDEN
LEICESTER SQUARE
HOLBORN
RUSSELL SQUARE
ALDWYCH
TEMPLE
BLACKFRIARS
MANSION HOUSE
CANNON STREET
MONUMENT FOR BANK
TOWER HILL
Fenchurch Street
LONDON BRIDGE
BOROUGH
WATERLOO
Waterloo & City Line
LAMBETH NORTH
ELEPHANT & CASTLE
KENNINGTON
OVAL
STOCKWELL
VAUXHALL
BRIXTON
CLAPHAM NORTH
CLAPHAM COMMON
CLAPHAM SOUTH
BALHAM
TOOTING BEC
TOOTING BROADWAY
COLLIERS WOOD
SOUTH WIMBLEDON
MORDEN
RIVER THAMES
HIGH BARNET
TOTTERIDGE & WHETSTONE
WOODSIDE PARK
MILL HILL EAST
WEST FINCHLEY
FINCHLEY CENTRAL
EAST FINCHLEY
HIGHGATE
ARCHWAY
TUFNELL PARK
KENTISH TOWN
CAMDEN ROAD
HOLLOWAY ROAD
CALEDONIAN ROAD
CALEDONIAN ROAD & BARNSBURY
KING'S CROSS ST PANCRAS
ANGEL
FARRINGDON
BARBICAN
MOORGATE
ST PAUL'S
CHANCERY LANE
BANK
LIVERPOOL STREET
BROAD STREET
OLD STREET
G.N. Electrics
ESCALATOR LINK
COCKFOSTERS
OAKWOOD
SOUTHGATE
ARNOS GROVE
BOUNDS GREEN
WOOD GREEN
TURNPIKE LANE
MANOR HOUSE
FINSBURY PARK
ARSENAL
TOTTENHAM HALE
SEVEN SISTERS
BLACKHORSE ROAD
WALTHAMSTOW CENTRAL
DRAYTON PARK
HIGHBURY & ISLINGTON
ESSEX ROAD
CANONBURY
DALSTON JUNCTION
BETHNAL GREEN
SHOREDITCH
ALDGATE EAST
ALDGATE
WHITECHAPEL
SHADWELL
WAPPING
ROTHERHITHE
SURREY DOCKS
NEW CROSS GATE
NEW CROSS
STEPNEY GREEN
MILE END
BOW ROAD
BROMLEY-BY-BOW
WEST HAM
PLAISTOW
UPTON PARK
EAST HAM
BARKING
UPNEY
BECONTREE
DAGENHAM HEATHWAY
DAGENHAM EAST
ELM PARK
HORNCHURCH
UPMINSTER BRIDGE
UPMINSTER
STRATFORD
LEYTON
LEYTONSTONE
SNARESBROOK
WANSTEAD
REDBRIDGE
GANTS HILL
SOUTH WOODFORD
WOODFORD
BUCKHURST HILL
LOUGHTON
DEBDEN
THEYDON BOIS
EPPING
NORTH WEALD
BLAKE HALL
ONGAR
RODING VALLEY
CHIGWELL
GRANGE HILL
HAINAULT
FAIRLOP
BARKINGSIDE
NEWBURY PARK
LINES
VICTORIA
CENTRAL
CIRCLE
PICCADILLY
NORTHERN
BAKERLOO
DISTRICT
METROPOLITAN
JUBILEE
BRITISH RAIL
Underground peaks only Main service-B.R.
Exhibition Service only
East London Section
Interchange with other Lines
Interchange with British Rail
Fenchurch Street Interchange with British Rail within walking distance
Open Mondays to Fridays, peak hours only
Closed on Sundays
Closed on Saturdays and Sundays
Certain stations are also closed on Public Holidays
Nearest stations for the Round London Sightseeing Tour
EUSTON Stations named in red have Travel Enquiry Offices
Piccadilly Line trains stop here early morning and late evening Mondays to Saturdays and all day Sundays